FAMILY ADVENTURE GUIDE™

MICHIGAN

"The Family Adventure Guide *series . . . enables parents to turn family travel into an exploration."*

—Alexandra Kennedy, Editor, *FamilyFun* magazine

MICHIGAN

FAMILY ADVENTURE GUIDE™

by

WILLIAM SEMION

A VOYAGER BOOK

The
Globe
Pequot
Press

OLD SAYBROOK, CONNECTICUT

Library of Congress Cataloging-in-Publication Data
Semion, William.
　　Family adventure guide : Michigan / by William Semion.
　　　　p. cm. — (Family adventure guide series)
　　"A Voyager book."
　　Includes index.
　　ISBN 1-56440-865-5
　　1. Michigan—Guidebooks. 2. Family recreation—Michigan—Guidebooks.
I. Title. II. Series.
F564.3.S46 1996
917.7404'43—dc20   96-15661
                                                              CIP

Manufactured in the United States of America
First Edition/Second Printing

ACKNOWLEDGMENTS

I wouldn't have tried and couldn't have succeeded in this endeavor without the support, encouragement, and suggestions of others. I shall be forever grateful to my wife, Kay, for helping me through some difficult times, teaching me more than she will ever realize, and inspiring my total love; to my research assistant, Scott Renas, for his digging; to Larry Keller, for turning me onto the path; to my father, Alex, for his direction; to my daughter, Sonya, and son, Justin, for checking phone numbers; and to my brother Al, my sister Sandra, and Dixie, for their support. Thanks also to Bob Brodbeck, for his camera work, and to James Richard, Laura Bollman, and Chris McElmeel. Thank you all. I love you.

MICHIGAN

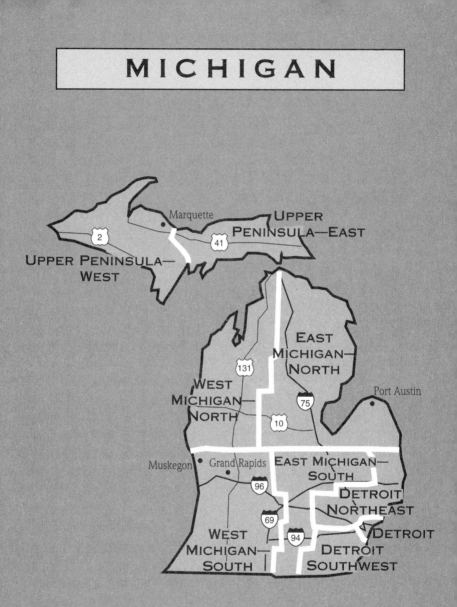

Upper Peninsula—East

Marquette

Upper Peninsula—West

East Michigan—North

Port Austin

West Michigan—North

Muskegon   Grand Rapids   East Michigan—South

Detroit Northeast

West Michigan—South   Detroit   Detroit Southwest

CONTENTS

INTRODUCTION

I have been fortunate. From the time I was old enough to remember, my parents loved to travel in Michigan. In fact, the Wolverine State was just about the only place they ever went. And I suspect that's true of a lot of us Michiganders. We just can't find a place to match the combination of attractions, both natural and otherwise, that our state offers.

I've seen Michigan in all her seasons, from the tip of the Keweenaw Peninsula in the north, dipped in autumn brilliance and summer greenery, to the Lake Erie shoreline on her south; from Lake Michigan's white sand beaches on her west, to the public fishing piers on her east; from her huge expanses of state and national forests, which number among the nation's largest tracts of publicly held land, to her fun-loaded cities with excitement for the family that's found nowhere else. This is someplace that stands up to the cliché "something for everyone."

One of my earliest memories is of crossing the Straits of Mackinac on one of the big ferryboats that took cars between the peninsulas as the Mackinac Bridge was being built. (Strange that the bridge, the island, the straits, and the county are spelled "Mackinac," but the city is "Mackinaw"—and that no one has been able to tell me why yet.) We spent a part of each summer along Lake Huron, frolicking on the beach and enjoying the lake's offerings, from perch fishing to driving its magnificent shoreline. We take our Great Lakes for granted. When foreigners or even those from other parts of the nation catch their first eyeful of Huron, Michigan, or, especially, mighty Superior, they're awestruck. And they grow incredulous when they realize that no, you really *can't* see across them. Did you know, for example, that Lake Michigan is generally more than 50 to 80 miles wide and more than 900 feet deep at its deepest point? And that scientists now think of Lake Superior, more than 1,000 feet deep, as more of a freshwater ocean than a lake?

When my wife, Kay, and I were raising our family, I was lucky to have a job that allowed me to continue my family's tradition of travel. Over the last twenty years, we've made it a point to introduce our children to the wonders that are found in our state so they, too, will have an appreciation someday of what Michigan offers the tourist. We've been on the road to somewhere in the state nearly every weekend since they were young, whether it be for viewing the brilliant foliage in the fall, skiing in winter, morel hunting in spring, or fishing the Great Lakes and exploring the high dunes and forested streams of our state parks in summer.

So many people rush outside their familiar surroundings to explore. They travel to Europe or the Caribbean. But it seems many never get around to discovering the delights in their own backyard. It's been estimated that fewer than half of all Michiganders have ever seen the span connecting the Upper and Lower Peninsulas, and when asked, many think the Mackinac Bridge goes to Mackinac Island instead.

I hope this book enlightens you, whether you're a Michigan resident or a first-time visitor who doesn't know Saginaw from Manistee—at least not yet. Through this book I hope to convince you of the bounty of activities that my state has to offer the family. And in the next pages, I've touched on only a sampling of the thousands of attractions you'll find. There are plenty more adventures awaiting you and your family if you're willing to explore and open new doors to discovery. Try a Michigan adventure or two, no matter the season. You'll learn more about our beautiful state and perhaps about yourself in the process. And by introducing your family to travel, you'll be helping them learn to appreciate the wonder all around them.

See you on the road!

The prices and rates listed in this guidebook were confirmed at press time. We recommend, however, that you call establishments to obtain current information before traveling.

Detroit Southwest

Only a few minutes' drive south and west of downtown Detroit's skyscrapers, you'll find one of the country's top universities nestled in a town that has attractions ranging from the offbeat to the educational. The region takes in Monroe, Washtenaw, and western Wayne Counties.

MONROE

It's party time on Lake Erie! Party boat time, that is. No, we're not talking about dancing and rock-and-roll bands. If the kids, or you, for that matter, have never gone fishing before, the perfect way to get hooked on the sport is aboard a boat that supplies everything from the rod to the bait to the expertise needed to find where the fish are biting.

Up to eight persons per trip climb aboard one of Captain Bill Currie's three stable, 30-foot craft and head out after walleye—the big brother to the perch that can top ten pounds each—in the waters of Lake Erie near Monroe, which has been termed the nation's walleye capital. Currie's boats, which are moored just off Interstate 75 at exit 11 (La Plaisance Road), at the Erie Party shop and docks just south of Monroe, make two trips into the lake's Michigan waters each day. The former U.S. Coast Guard search-and-rescue expert now scours the lake for schools of the voracious fish, which will hit lures like the Erie Dearie, generally tipped with either a juicy nightcrawler or fat minnow, depending on the time of year.

If you've never fished, you're in luck. The $60-per-person tab includes use of a fully rigged rod. Bait's included too, and you can keep your catch in the boat's cooler until you get ashore. All that's needed for an angler over age sixteen is a one-day or an annual Michigan fishing license, available at the dock

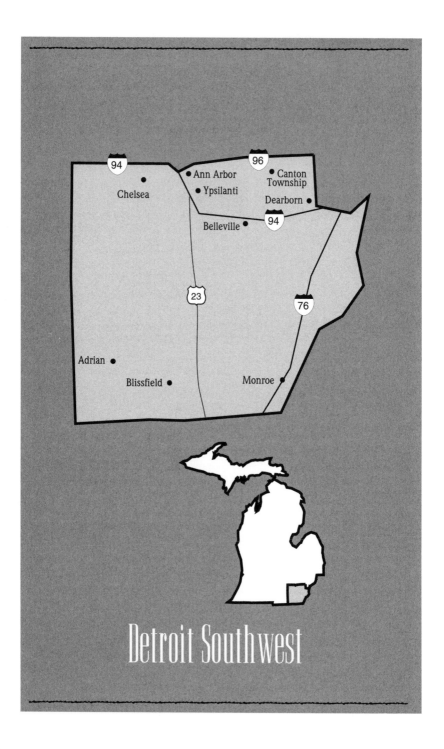

Detroit Southwest

for a small fee. Take along a cooler full of drink—no alcohol aboard, please—and you're ready for action

Once Currie reaches a "hot area," he shuts off the engines and tells you to lower your bait. Rather than anchoring in one spot, he usually fishes by the drift method for the hundreds of thousands of fish that inhabit this lake, which once was declared to be "dead" after decades of abuse. And Currie will know when he's found a hot spot by the football-shaped blips on his computerized fish-finder. Walleyes are usually found near the bottom, so look at the finder to spot 'em and the captain will tell you how many seconds to let the bait sink. Two tips for best catches: "jig" (raise and lower) your fishing rod often to attract fish, and try to cast your line on the windward side of the boat. That way it will freely drift past your quarry, rather than being tugged under the vessel first. Be alert for that first telltale tug of a lunker walleye mouthing the bait and then set the hook. But be careful; walleyes have tender mouths. Reel steadily and don't apply too much pressure or the hook might pull out. Currie will be there to net your catch and urge you on to take your limit of six big ones. For charter information on his twice-daily runs, call **Currie's Tradewind Charters** at (313) 243–2319. Your money will be refunded in case of bad weather.

CARLETON

Where does milk really come from? Do brown cows give chocolate milk? And how do cream, sugar, and a lot of hard work become all those luscious flavors of ice cream at the local store? Answer all your kids' questions and more with a visit to the **Calder Dairy Farm** near Carleton in Monroe County, south of Detroit. The maker of out-of-this-world chocolate milk and holiday eggnog so thick it's like liquid ice cream, milk that's still sold in glass bottles, and twenty-two flavors of ice cream has opened its farm for tours to show kids and others how the milk that's in your fridge gets there. They'll see up close that no, it doesn't just come from the back room of the corner market.

Your family can stroll the 180-acre farm to see and pet the holstein and Brown Swiss cows during the 4:00 P.M. daily milking of the herd of sixty-five. Electric machines are used to milk the animals every twelve hours, which doesn't leave much leisuretime for farmers like the Calders. Each cow usually provides up to sixty-five pounds of milk at a session, enough to fill seven and a half one-gallon jugs. The raw product is then transported to **Calder's Dairy** and retail store at 1020 Southfield Road in Lincoln Park, a southwestern Detroit suburb, where it's pasteurized and bottled as either homogenized or "cream line-style" milk. Elsewhere on the farm kids can see and pet more than a hundred other animals, such as waddling ducks and honking geese. They can hop aboard

Everyone gets into the act when fishing for walleye on Lake Erie in Monroe, the nation's walleye capital.

a real hay wagon hitched to huge, stately Belgian horses for a trip to see even more exotic species, like llamas, squawking peacocks, and fallow deer. They'll also learn that pigs aren't as dirty as they've read, and they can touch sheep's wool on the hoof to feel that it's actually a bit sticky from its rich lanolin.

Visits to the farm are free. Afterward, take your gang to the small on-site store, where they can sink their teeth into a huge Calder ice-cream cone. You can also head to the main store, where, as they walk inside, kids can watch as the milk flows through pipes from trucks for processing into everything from cottage cheese to old-fashioned buttermilk. To find the farm, take Telegraph Road to South Stony Creek Road. Head west about 5 miles to Fenzel Road; then go south and watch for the signs. For more information, call (313) 654–2622.

ADRIAN AND BLISSFIELD

Take the family aboard the world's only life-size toy train and then introduce the kids to the way small-town life used to be—but with all the stores and other comforts of the present—in the next-door-neighbor cities of **Adrian** and **Blissfield** in southeastern Michigan.

Settled in 1826 by a railroad tycoon and his family, Adrian, nicknamed the City of Maples because of its downtown greenery, was the site of the first railroad in Michigan. An extension of the old Erie & Kalamazoo line ran from Toledo, Ohio, then called Port Lawrence, north to here. When the last strips of iron rail were laid in 1836, the line became the first west of Schenectady, New York, and one of the nation's first. Horses pulled the cars initially, and the line scored another breakthrough when the first steam engine west of the Alleghenies took over a year later, in 1837, the year Michigan became a state. A round-trip ticket meant spending an entire day aboard.

Neighboring Blissfield was settled about the same time and remains Michigan's biggest village. If you're heading here during the holidays, step aboard the 1940s-era, air-conditioned-and-heated coaches of the **Adrian & Blissfield Railroad** at the Blissfield East depot, downtown along U.S. 223. Your kids will be amazed as the world's only full-size Lionel diesel engine, painted just like the toy trains produced by Lionel, enters the station. Then they'll sit back and be treated to a ninety-minute trip through the countryside past manicured, tilled farm fields and over at least two old trestles crossing the Raisin River. If they're especially vigilant, they might even see a deer or two. Themed rides take place throughout the year. During the winter holidays Santa himself makes an appearance on every trip in December to take toy orders from the kids. A special "Ghost Train" appears during the two weeks before Halloween and features ghosts and goblins on board as well as ghoulish sights along the tracks.

Everyone's in for a special treat on certain Fridays, when the line adds a murder mystery to solve aboard. On Fridays, Saturdays, and selected Sundays at other times of the year, the train turns into a restaurant on rails, serving up to a hundred persons dinner on china and linen in two dining cars, with choice of prime rib, fresh salmon, or chicken, with soup, salad, and dessert. All the food is catered by Blissfield's **Hathaway House** restaurant.

After you ride the rails, stroll downtown Blissfield's main street, a browser's delight lined with shops that during the holidays are especially festive. In the **Old Country Store** crafters mall, nearly eighty local artisans sell their wares, from hand-sewn quilts to tree ornaments. Other downtown shops specialize in crafts too. Kids can hunt for presents for mom and dad and then meet up with you for a treat at the old-fashioned soda fountain in the Old Country Store. The area also is a hotbed for antiques hunters, with the five year-round antiques malls hosting hundreds of dealers. Return another time to dine in the Hathaway House, a beautifully restored 1850s mansion. Or if the kids are in the mood for burgers, head in the back to the former carriage house, now the **Main Street Stable and Tavern.** In Adrian, catch a play at the 1866 **Croswell Opera House,** one of the state's best local theaters, or introduce the youngsters to the **Adrian Symphony,** one of the most successful small-town symphonies in the nation. Both towns are along U.S. 223, reached off U.S. 23, north and west of Monroe. For information on train schedules, call (517) 486–5979; or the Hathaway House, (517) 486–2141; and on the general area, (800) 536–2933.

CHELSEA

Such a deal! The kids think you'll be taking them on another one of your educational tours. It's that, yes, but there's a special treat at the end that will make them eager to learn how grain is made into the flour that makes the brownies, cakes, and muffins at the **Chelsea Milling Company,** a landmark in this friendly rural town just west of Ann Arbor, off Interstate 94.

Big cities in the East and other regions may have their skyscrapers, but in the Midwest's farm country, the tall spires you'll see on the horizons of most towns are the grain silos, and that's true for this town in the middle of southern Michigan's farm belt. It just had to be that something good would come from them, and since 1930 the silos and grain-grinding machines at the Chelsea Milling Company have been producing seventeen varieties of baking mixes, from morning muffins speckled with blueberries to luscious brownies and the first all-purpose baking flour.

The Chelsea Milling Company began when "Grandma Mabel" Holmes came up with the idea of a flour that's ready to use for making pancakes, biscuits, and other goodies without having to mix all the ingredients first. Today as many as 14,000 persons a year–split between children and adults–stroll through the plant where Jiffy All-Purpose Baking Flour and sixteen other products are produced.

Tours of the facility last up to two hours, depending on the size of the crowd. First you'll be treated to a slide show that starts with a history of the company and how Grandma Mabel's idea in 1930 launched the Jiffy line of mixes. Kids can learn the entire flour-making process, including how the company's milling rollers separate the wheat from the chaff by removing the husk from the raw Michigan grain and sifting lighter and smaller materials from heavier and larger ones. The wheat is ground and rolled about a dozen times; then the resulting flour is bleached, enriched with vitamins, and, according to company vice president Dudley Holmes, aged for about a week. Holmes says that virtually nothing is wasted. The "middlings," everything that isn't flour, is sold to animal feed companies and the bran is sold to Kellogg's in Battle Creek to make cereal. The slide show over, tour guides then take you to the packaging operations, where you'll see boxes made and filled with what's being produced that day, everything from corn muffin mix to pizza dough. Holmes reports that the company processes a staggering 450,000 pounds of flour, filling 1.4 million—that's million—boxes a day under the Jiffy label, for stores in all fifty states and military bases around the world.

Last stop on the tour is a treat for both adults and kids. Grown-ups receive a free package of muffin, cake, or frosting mix and a recipe booklet, while the kids can latch onto a box of brownie mix or pizza dough that they can take with them and bake at home. (Sorry, but the company's best-seller, corn muffin mix, isn't included.)

Afterward, explore downtown Chelsea's shops, the former-railroad-depot-turned-local-history-museum, and restaurants like the pressed-tin-ceilinged **Common Grill;** and if it's open, take in a performance at the **Purple Rose Theater.** Who knows? You might even see Chelsea resident and Hollywood actor Jeff Daniels, who's starred in such varying roles as Harry in *Dumb and Dumber* and a Union hero in the movie epic *Gettysburg.* After all, he is part owner. To find Chelsea, head west from Ann Arbor on Interstate 94, take the Chelsea exit, and head north. You'll soon see the company's silos. The theater is nearby on Park Street. Chelsea Milling Company's free tours take place Monday through Friday between 8:30 A.M. and 1:30 P.M.; call (313) 475–1361 for reservations. For current information about Purple Rose Theater productions, call (313) 475–7902. Occasional productions may be too intense for children under sixteen, so ask before making reservations.

ANN ARBOR

What's as tall as a house and has rows of huge, sharp teeth? What animal that's a cousin of the elephant once roamed Michigan and other parts of the United States? Ever see a real Egyptian mummy? You'll find the mummy's tomb, minus the curse, dinosaurs straight out of *Jurassic Park,* plus a lot more finds worthy of

Indiana Jones himself at the **University of Michigan Museums** in Ann Arbor.

Hundreds of families come here, especially on weekends, to entertain and teach their children at the exhibits at two museums. First on the list to visit should be the **Exhibit Museum of Natural History,** a treasure of prehistoric Michigan and other discoveries that will appeal especially to kids. The museum has hundreds of individual displays, but the main exhibit hall is what excites kids the most. In the dimly lit hall, they'll come across the fossilized bones of a snarling allosaurus standing over its "kill," a fossilized stegosaurus like those that roamed the earth millions of years ago and were unearthed near Cleveland, Utah. At another exhibit, they can stand next to a skeleton of a huge, elephantlike 10,000-year-old mastodon that was found in a Michigan farmer's field near Owosso.

When it opened in 1994, kids were lined up into the street to be the first to view the long, deadly claws of the museum's newest exhibit: a deinonychus, a relative of the velociraptors of *Jurassic Park* fame. Other exhibits presented through dioramas create a picture of what Michigan was like at various times through prehistory and what you might find in the region's forests and ponds today. There is also a planetarium presenting weekend shows.

At the well-stocked museum store, kids can take home smaller model versions or books giving more details about what they saw inside, or they can go home wearing a velociraptor T-shirt.

A few blocks away, near the Michigan Union Building on South State Street, say "hi" to Djheutymosc, a real mummy, at the **Kelsey Museum of Archaeology.** Scientists who examined it discerned that he was a former priest who lived in southern Egypt sometime between 685 and 525 B.C. Museum visitors might be surprised at seeing the mummy of a cat (felines were revered as gods in ancient Egypt and were often entombed with humans to keep them company in the afterlife), as well as other artifacts unearthed during university "digs."

The Museum of Art features Near Eastern and Far Eastern, African, and Western art from the sixth century to the present. Then it's on to the twentieth century and beyond at the **Phoenix Memorial Laboratory** on the north side of Ann Arbor, where the university's research mini–nuclear reactor is housed. All of the university's museums are free and open to the public. The Exhibit Museum is at Geddes Road and North University; for information call (313) 764–0478. Hours are Monday through Saturday from 9:00 A.M. to 5:00 P.M. and Sunday from 1:00 to 5:00 P.M. The Kelsey Museum is at 434 South State and is open from 9:00 A.M. to 4:00 P.M. during the week and from 1:00 to 4:00 P.M. on the weekend (313–764–9304); the Museum of Art is at 525 South State and is open from 10:00 A.M. to 5:00 P.M., Monday through

BILL'S TOP FAMILY ADVENTURES IN DETROIT SOUTHWEST

1. Walleye fishing on Lake Erie with Bill Currie's Tradewinds Charters, Monroe
2. University of Michigan Museums and Hands-On Museum, Ann Arbor
3. Yankee Air Force Museum, Ypsilanti
4. Greenfield Village and Henry Ford Museum, Dearborn

Saturday, and from noon to 5:00 P.M. on Sunday (313–764–0395). For directions to the Phoenix Lab, on the university's North Campus, call for (313) 764–6220 and arrange for a guided tour.

Ann Arbor's **Hands-On Museum** is a museum kids will love. One of the state's oldest museums catering to children of all ages, it's a place where, as one eleven-year-old noted, kids can learn and have fun at the same time. Where else could they have the opportunity to look inside a living beehive? Or peer into a mirror while riding a stationary bike and actually see a skeleton move as they do?

Opened in 1982 in the city's renovated red Central Fire House—the new one's just down the street—the Hands-On Museum contains four floors of fun and has proved so popular that it recently expanded into the building next door. That colorful section is devoted to tots, who can develop their motor skills and at the same time start on the road to discovery about how things work.

In the main museum, each floor is divided into subject areas. The first floor teaches kids about their bodies and how they work. Among other things, they can measure their own heart rate and try to beat the clock to measure their reaction time. In a special room a strobe light flashes and kids are amazed as their own shadows are captured on the opposite wall.

Climb the stairs to the second floor to learn about physics and nature, from how to build an arch and exploring fossils to seeing the aforementioned bees, busy as, well, bees, preparing their plastic-encased hive. (Kids can even follow the workers as they head outside and return via a clear plastic tube.) On the third floor, while exploring light and optics, they'll marvel at a hologram and see the tricks a strobe light can play on the eye, and on the fourth floor they'll try out a computer or find out what really happens when they flush a toilet. Explanations are provided for everything, but they're mostly ignored by the kids, who often seem to flit from one exhibit to another, just having fun and not really knowing or caring that they're actually learning something.

The museum also draws kids in through unique programs such as overnight camp-ins, birthday party programs, and special workshops and weekend activities that range from maze making to exploring potential careers. One event teaches youngsters how rocks are formed by doing something every youngster likes: baking chocolate-chip cookies. The museum is at the corner of Fifth and Huron. From U.S. 23, take Main Street south to Huron and turn left. Hours are Tuesday through Friday from 10:00 A.M. to 5:30 P.M., Saturday from 10:00 A.M. to 5:00 P.M., and Sunday afternoon from 1:00 to 5:00 P.M. Admission is $2.50 for students and seniors and $4.00 for others; call (313) 995–5439.

Another popular attraction draws thousands of families to Ann Arbor each year. It may be crowded at times, it may be noisy, and it may be occasionally offbeat, but it's fun for the entire family. It's the **Ann Arbor Art Fairs,** an annual gathering of more than a thousand artists, who take over downtown for four days in the third week of July.

Although the event is collectively known as "the art fair," there are actually three simultaneous art festivals. The city's downtown virtually closes to auto traffic for four days as an estimated 120,000-plus enjoy one of the country's largest summer art events. Special events every day cater to families with kids, from tots on up. Discounts offered by merchants eager to draw in the crowds will lure teens to record stores like **Schoolkids** and **Tower Records,** while other retailers hold huge sidewalk sales for bargain hunters.

But back to the art fairs. To get your bearings, think of Ann Arbor as having three downtowns, one along Main Street, another around State Street, near the University of Michigan's classrooms, and the third along South University on the southern edge of the campus. The original, juried art fest is the **Ann Arbor Street Art Fair,** in the heart of the University of Michigan campus, on South University and East University avenues and Church Street. It celebrated its thirty-sixth anniversary in 1995.

The twenty-nine-year-old **State Street Art Fair** runs the length of the State Street shopping district and has grown so large that it's spilled over into four surrounding streets. The **Summer Art Fair** is spread out along Main Street and adjoining avenues. While it's been known as more commercial in years past, it's come a long way in the past few summers. While the three fairs may be separate, each flows into the other, which makes walking the entire area easy. Artists booths are set up down the middle of each street, with passages wide enough for wheelchairs and strollers despite the crowds. Only a few tents ask that children be carried, owing to cramped quarters. As you peruse the artwork, you'll find everything from original pottery and woven clothing to wildlife art and photography. If your teens are into beads, they'll find plenty, along with amulets for make-your-own necklaces. At the Ann Arbor Street Art Fair, face paint experts deftly design flowers, flags, and hundreds of other forms on willing young faces, and youngsters can even try their own hand at the easel with watercolors. There's a free family art activity center at the Summer Art Fair, too, with lots of chances for kids to create the next art craze.

Much of the entertainment isn't at the booths, however. At intersections between each fair and along the expanse of grass and diagonal sidewalks along State known as the "diag," magicians, jugglers, and other street buskers love to coax child "assistants" from the crowds they draw, and the kids love it too. For more information, contact the Ann Arbor Street Art Fair at (313) 994–5260, the State Street Art Fair at (313) 663–6511, and the Summer Art Fair at (313) 662–ARTS.

When the kids get hungry after all this walking, there's plenty of food, from Korean to Greek, at the fair, but steer your family through the crowds to a city institution at 410 East Liberty. **Le Dog** is an unpretentious red take-out stand with two ordering windows—an eatery that only wanted to be a hot dog stand when it started 17 years go, according to owner/chef Jules VanDyck-Dobos, and now has something for kids as well as for adults with a more educated palate, too.

"I really wanted to call it 'Lemonade and Hot Dogs,' but it was too long for the sign, so we trimmed it to 'Le Dog,'" he explains. But hot dogs apparently weren't enough for this eclectic city, and VanDyck-Dobos soon introduced a bit more exotic fare: cuisine brought back from his travels in the off-season–he closes during the coldest months, when his little place is too frosty–to his native Europe and elsewhere (VanDyck-Dobo's family moved to Ann Arbor after the abortive 1956 Hungarian revolt, his father to teach at the University of Michigan.) He now serves everything from lobster bisque and bouillabaisse to New Orleans–style jambalaya. Treat your kids to one of LeDog's famous triple-chocolate shakes, or clear your palate with the newest offering, Italian ices. To get to Ann Arbor's campus area, take the State Street exit north off Interstate 94.

The low-slung headquarters of the Domino's Pizza chain may not be in the museum business anymore, showing off owner Tom Monaghan's classic-car collection, but families will find a whole slew of other things to do at **Domino's Farms,** which hosts special events throughout the year that spell family fun.

Located next to the Frank Lloyd Wright–inspired headquarters in Ann Arbor, Domino's Farms is meant to depict a Michigan farm of the early 1900s, and it hosts a plethora of programs geared to youngsters of all ages.

Come Easter, for instance, there's an annual egg hunt for the wee ones, with up to 1,500 eager youngsters divided into four age groups and loosed to scour the grounds for plastic eggs that contain candy, stickers or coupons redeemable for age-appropriate prizes such as mugs and beach towels. And of course there's a visit by the Easter bunny, as well as face painting, hayrides, clowns, and other entertainment.

In summer kids can ride a hay wagon to view a herd of twenty buffalo in a fenced area. If your children are able to spot the sometimes shy animals, wait to see the look in their eyes when you tell them the woolly beasts can weigh as much as the family car and can run nearly as fast.

In the petting farm area, kids are encouraged to stroke the chickens, sheep, goats, peacocks, potbellied pigs, and horses, from an American minia-ture to one of the largest, a Belgian. Events appealing to the older set include arts-and-craft shows and annual classic-car exhibitions (call for a schedule).

In winter Domino's is the site of one of the largest outdoor light shows in the state, and your family can become a part of it. More than 600,000 lights strung throughout the complex create a symphony of color against snowy fields in beautiful displays. Kids will marvel at webs of lights shaped like ani-mals, climbing up trees to create living statues, and arching over your car as you travel the roads in the complex, passing through tunnels of illumination that spell out festive holiday messages. The entry fee of about $5.00 per car helps pay the electricity bill and what's left over goes to charity. In 1994 more than 42,000 carloads enjoyed the show, which runs from the day before Thanksgiving to December 31. Domino's Farms is easily reached by exiting U.S. 23 at Ann Arbor–Plymouth Road, turning east, and following the signs. For dates of other activities, call (313) 930–5032.

The Ann Arbor Convention and Visitors Bureau (313–995–7281) has more information on what to see and do and on where to stay in this city that's been called the most zestful in southeastern Michigan.

YPSILANTI

What began in 1981 as a way to remember Michigan's role in World War II and in America's aviation history has grown into a major family attraction at the **Yankee Air Force Museum,** just east of Ypsilanti, only a ten-minute drive east of Ann Arbor.

Located at Willow Run Airport, which in World War II was the home of the Ford Motor Company's giant Willow Run bomber plant (at one time the world's largest factory under one roof), the museum features twenty-one restored

ANNUAL EVENTS FOR THE FAMILY IN DETROIT SOUTHWEST

Wayne County Air Show, late May and early June, Willow Run Airport, (313) 482–8888

National Strawberry Festival, mid-June, Belleville, (313) 697–3137

Ann Arbor Art Fairs, mid-July, Ann Arbor, (313) 995–7281

Greenfield Village festivals, September through April, Dearborn, (313) 271–1620

Domino's Farms Christmas Light Display, Thanksgiving through early January, Domino's Farms, (313) 930–5032

military aircraft, many of them flyable. It's located in a wooden hangar that served as a school for mechanics when B-24 "Liberator" bombers were produced here.

At its height, you'll learn, the facility employed more than 40,000 workers, who turned out one B-24 every fifty-nine minutes. While seeing a B-24 is rare these days (the museum is still searching for one; there are only twelve known in the world), air buffs in your family can examine craft like a B-25 Mitchell, the type of bomber used in General Jimmy Doolittle's historic Tokyo raid. It's the only flying example in the United States. Outside, kids can see a giant B-52D jet bomber and by appointment can even climb inside. Other craft include Korean War–era jets, trainers, and the newest addition, a rare flyable B-17 bomber, named the *Yankee Lady,* which was restored over a nine-year period by museum volunteers.

If you think there's nothing here for girls, think again. Inside, the "Women in Aviation" room details the contributions of Amelia Earhart and other pioneers, and also relates the untold story of Army Air Force WASPs, who ferried planes across the oceans during the war.

Don't forget to visit the gift shop for logo gear like hats and sweatshirts, plus videos and more. You can also research your favorite craft at the aerospace library, which preserves flight manuals, vintage magazines, and aircraft photos.

Each spring, around Memorial Day, the YAFM welcomes visitors to an open house during the big **Wayne County Air Show** at Willow Run, which fills two afternoons and always includes appearances by thrilling precision flight teams, wing walkers, aerobats, and other aviators. On the ground, displays and tours let junior pilots peer inside military and civilian aircraft.

To reach the museum from Interstate 94, exit at Belleville Road and go north to Tyler Road; then turn west, drive to Beck Road, and turn north. Go about ¾ of a mile and you'll spot a sign for the museum on the left. Guided tours are available for groups of ten or more (two weeks' reservation notice is usually required). Call (313) 483–4030 for current information about admission fees and hours of operation.

Like a real version of TV's *Green Acres,* **Wiard's Orchards** is just outside Ypsilanti, only minutes west of downtown Ann Arbor. The farm has been in the Wiard family since 1853, has cackling pheasants, bleating sheep, strutting peacocks, and places where kids can jump into hay piles, hop aboard a "train" for a trip through an orchard, and then dance their achy-breaky hearts out to twangy country music.

Each weekend in October up to 15,000 persons head for Wiard's for its annual **Country Fair Weekends.** The Wiards had been running a quiet orchard, growing apples, peaches, and other fruit, when one family member thought it'd be nice to open a roadside market. Then came the fair idea, and before they knew it they had a family hit on their hands.

Kids are catered to farm-wide, with goats, pigs, and chickens to feed, ponies to ride, and eager helpers ready to paint young faces. Two "trains" (actually converted trucks) take families on orchard tours past trees heavy with fruit and fields of ripe pumpkins. Kids get a kick out of yanking apples right off the tree and picking out candidates for their Halloween jack-o-lanterns.

An arts-and-crafts fair will tempt Mom and Dad, and they can even try out those new country dance steps in front of a live band. Next stop: glasses of fresh-squeezed cider. Then head for the bakery or the butcher shop, where you can buy everything from a burger to a side of beef. And the strong-hearted can walk through two haunted barns—a tame version for tots and a heavy-duty model for teens and adults. On certain weekends the farm features military themes, such as Civil War and Revolutionary War encampments, with participants living as soldiers of each era.

"We like to provide plenty of family fun so you can come out and not have to spend a lot of money," says Jay Wiard. Most events are free. There's a $5.00 per car charge. Wiard's is at 5565 Merritt Road. Take Whitaker Road, exit 183 off Interstate 94 near Ypsilanti, and travel 2 miles south to the blinking light. Then follow Stony Creek Road south about 2 miles, turn right on Merritt, and follow the signs. Phone (313) 482–7744 for an events update.

BELLEVILLE

How many restaurants can offer the chance for families to enjoy an inexpensive lakeside meal and be only a few steps away from the night's entertainment too? **Reflections Lakeside,** in the town of Belleville, about 5 miles east of Ypsilanti, does both. Looking over beautiful Belleville Lake, a dammed portion of the Huron River, it's a perfect, inexpensive spot for everyone, especially if you prefer restaurants that don't serve alcohol.

Reflections' dinner menu runs the gamut from American prime rib to Mexican tacos to fish. A fish combination plate, including shrimp, catfish, cod, and smelt with hush puppies on the side, is only $7.95. Want chicken instead? A charbroiled chicken breast with shrimp is just $8.75. And barbecued ribs, a specialty, are priced at just $12.95 for a two-person portion, $8.45 for a half-slab, and $6.45 for the slightly smaller "special." A kid's menu features a choice of the standby burger, chicken strips, spaghetti, hot dog, grilled cheese, or fish and chips for $2.95, including drink and dessert. All adult dinners come with salad or soup, potato, and vegetables.

Save room for dessert and take the kids down the wheelchair-accessible ramp or the stairs to the ice-cream bar on the lower level. That's where the real fun begins. After you decide on a bowl or a cone and settle on one of the flavors from Northville's Guernsey Dairy, grab a bag of fish food and head outside to the docks. You'll soon realize that they weren't just built for hungry boaters. For as soon as you walk out on a dock, not only do the ducks come calling for handouts, but the water starts boiling as literally hundreds of pounds of huge, bugle-mouthed carp come calling for a morsel. Join in with the crowds of tots, teens, and others who stand openmouthed as the fish pile onto one another and beg for the food pellets. Mallard ducks competing for the food will walk on top of the writhing masses of carp to reach a morsel before the fish get to them. Fish mouths stick straight out of the water, opening and closing as each tries to grab a piece before another. And as if on some signal, the show's over once you run out of food. Even for longtime anglers who'd never want to catch a carp, it's a sight not to be missed. The fish are there year-round but need more coaxing to come out of the depths in cold-weather months. Reflections Lakeside is at 146 High Street in downtown Belleville. Exit Interstate 94 at Belleville Road, turn south, and take the first right after the bridge over the lake. The restaurant opens at 7:00 A.M.; call (313) 697–2511.

Come Father's Day weekend, the farm fields around this part of southern Lower Michigan blush bright red, as one of the state's most luscious crops comes into its prime time. It's strawberry-picking time, and two farms offering pick-your-own family fun each welcome as many as 10,000 pickers annually during the two to three weeks of the season, which is highlighted by Belleville's **National Strawberry Festival.**

The **Rowe Farm,** with twenty-seven acres of berries offers row upon row of the luscious fruit over the picking season—some of the largest strawberries you'll ever have the pleasure of sprinkling with sugar and plopping into a bowl full of cream before savoring every bite to finish off a summer meal.

Tradition among many longtime berry pickers says that the choice is best in the mornings, so the farm opens with the sun still low on the horizon. There's a practical reason too: It's hot out there in the afternoon! Berries are sold by the pound, now around 75 cents, and considering their size, it doesn't take long before you and your kids are lugging four or five pounds of the beautiful, ripe red treats up to the weigh-in center. Of course, that's after you have sampled a berry, or maybe two, in the field. You have to, you know. Never know when you might end up in a row with funny-tasting berries, so you have to test at least one from each, right? And the kids have to get in their share of testing, too. Rrriiight.

The picking, though, is just a prelude to the National Strawberry Festival, which each year draws up to a hundred thousand berry lovers to Belleville over the weekend and closes downtown to traffic. Organizers pride themselves on making the entire festival a family affair, with lots of kids events and even a family circus. At games designated especially for young children, players can win prizes by reaching for a plastic duck, blowing the biggest bubble gum bubble, or joining in a tug-of-war. There are pony rides and places where young hands can make arts-and-crafts items. Carnival rides at two locations include a special section just for the youngest. The big Saturday parade features more than two hundred units. At Saint Anthony's Church you'll find an old-fashioned family circus under the big top, with jugglers, clowns, and other performers who delight in plunging into the audience and involving the children in the fun.

And, of course, there are strawberry treats everywhere you turn, from shortcake and pies to sundaes. Whatever they can put strawberries in, they do. Fresh strawberries also are sold by the quart or case, in case you got to the party to late too join the picking.

During the fun families can relax on a cruise on Belleville Lake aboard the paddle wheeler *Princess Laura,* which takes on passengers at the Reflections Restaurant dock. Evening cruises include dinner, and moonlight trips feature music and dancing. From Interstate 94 take the Belleville Road exit and turn south into town. There's free parking at the Wayne County fairgrounds, with shuttle rides to the festival; for festival information call (313) 697-3137. The farm is within only a few minutes of downtown. For picking information call Rowe's at (313) 482-8538. For cruise information call (313) 699-8921.

CANTON TOWNSHIP

Head north a few miles to Canton Township. Along Ford Road, the main drag in this suburban Detroit bedroom community, is probably one of the best, if not the best, public clubs for racquet sports in the state. If you want to introduce your kids to a sport they can play virtually the rest of their lives, **Rose Shores Racquetball and Fitness Center** is the place to show them how to play squash, racquetball, or an old American standard, paddleball (it's slower than the others but requires more accuracy).

The equipment each type of game requires may be different, but it's all light enough that players of all ages can try it out. The object is always the same: Hit it hard or soft, low or high, straight or angled, just be sure it stays in bounds and that your opponent can't return a shot to do the same to you. If a game is still too far in the future for some, there's a playroom with toys and other entertainment for younger kids. You'll often see a father or mother on at least one court teaching a son or daughter the fundamentals of the game—number one of which is not hitting your opponent with the ball or your racquet and always exhibiting good sportsmanship.

Several times throughout the fall, summer, and spring, Rose Shores hosts daylong sports parties, where for about $10 your kids can find others their own age and skill level to play in the so-called challenge court, round-robin games in which the winner stays on to play all comers. If they only want to watch, there are four courts with back walls of shatterproof glass.

Rose Shores also has two lounges for groups who want to complete their visit with a meal or snack, including facilities to keep a pizza or other food you pack at home hot or cold. The large and never busy fitness center lets kids as young as ten work out under a parent's supervision on more than a dozen Nautilus weight machines. A new feature added in 1996 is a family fun center with a dedicated play area, children's activities, aerobics, and karate instruction.

If you want to try impress your kids with your prowess, come on a Friday evening or Sunday morning for the open-to-any-ability-or-age challenge courts. Together you will learn a lot from the hotshots and the sandbaggers during these two- to three-hour round-robin affairs, and you'll meet new friends, too. If your children have never experienced a sauna or steam bath—a great place to recuperate after a match—both the men's and the women's locker rooms have them. Rose Shores is open from mid-September through early May and is located at 41677 Ford Road. Exit Interstate 275 at Ford Road and head west about a quarter-mile. The building is on the south side, set back from the road. To reserve a court, call (313) 981–3080.

DEARBORN

About a mile south and then east about 10 more miles is Dearborn, the city that Henry Ford built where there are two museums dedicated to what Ford admired most—middle America. But the **Henry Ford Museum** and **Greenfield Village** today are much more than what Ford had envisioned when the complex opened in the 1930s.

From the car in which President John Kennedy rode in Dallas on November 22, 1963, and the chair President Abraham Lincoln sat in at Ford's Theater on April 14, 1865, to the tiny clapboard bicycle shop in Ohio where two brothers taught the world how to fly, this gathering of more than a hundred historic buildings and one of the world's great museums makes the ninety-three-acre complex in Dearborn one of the state's top family tourist destinations.

At the entrance to the grounds stands the Henry Ford Museum, surrounded by the Ford Motor Company. The building itself is a look-alike of Philadelphia's Independence Hall. Inside, your family will be drawn to Kennedy's Lincoln Continental convertible, part of a permanent display called "The Automobile in American Life." Besides that bit of touching nostalgia, be sure to take the youngsters, who may have possibly never seen a drive-in, to the miniversion showing old film clips. It's right next to the full-size old-fashioned service station. Peer inside a real New York diner and one of the first rooms of what then was a new motel chain, Holiday Inns. Walk past the museum's collection of more than a hundred antique and classic cars, including the only remaining 1896 Duryea, America's first production vehicle. And wait until the kids stand dwarfed next to the giant, 600-ton steam locomotive. The museum's newest exhibit highlights Motown music (see page 37).

Greenfield Village is dedicated to the history of American inventiveness. See where the Wright brothers designed their first airplane and where they lived. Then step into the laboratory where Thomas Edison invented the lightbulb. Edison's chair remains just as the inventor left it. That's because it was nailed to the floor by his friend Henry Ford when Edison visited to celebrate his most famous invention's fiftieth anniversary. Recent additions have remembered the nation's African American community too. A log cabin is similar to the one in which scientist, inventor, and teacher George Washington Carver grew up, an other exhibit depicts how African Americans lived both before and after slavery.

Let's not leave out the restaurants. If you want to show the kids what an 1850s stagecoach stop may have looked like, head to the Eagle Tavern, where you can sample fare of the era and be greeted as if you are city slickers just off the stage, right down to the comments about those "strange city clothes" you're wearing. It's one of six restaurants in the complex. Take a carriage or steamboat ride in summer, or if you visit in winter, a horse-drawn sleigh when

Just a few of the historic vehicles you can see when you visit the Henry Ford Museum, in Dearborn. (Courtesy Henry Ford Museum and Greenfield Village)

the snow cooperates. The village and museum are at 20900 Oakwood Boulevard. From Interstate 94, exit to the Southfield Freeway (Michigan 39) northbound and go 3 miles to northbound Oakwood, then go 2 more miles to the entrance. The admission charge is $12.50 for adults, $11.50 for seniors ages sixty-two and over, and $6.25 for kids ages five to twelve. Phone (313)

271–1620 for details about special events, like the antique auto muster, sheep shearing at Firestone Farm, and more.

If your kid's an expert at a Vulcan mind meld, if you're fluent in the imaginary language of the Klingon Empire, or if you enjoy dressing up like a Star Fleet admiral or other such mythical character, plot a course to the Dearborn Civic Center, 15801 Michigan Avenue, each spring and summer for the **Star Trek Convention.**

Even if your family members are just casual fans, it's a great spot to people watch. You'll see all kinds here at the state's largest trekkie confab: parents dressed as Kirk and Spock from the original television and movie series, teens masquerading as Worf or Riker from *The Next Generation,* and children dressed like Commander Benjamin Cisco of "Deep Space 9." There will probably even be a contingent wearing the latest Janeway or Nelix uniforms from the newest sci-fi series to go where no one's gone before, *Star Trek Voyager,* and kids done up as young Ensign Crusher (from *Next Generation,* for the unenlightened) or other aspiring junior officers. Some fans who can't stay away have even been known to tote their week-old babies, garbed appropriately in Federation uniforms.

Hard to believe that all this started when two New York high-school kids fascinated with science fiction decided to become the youngest convention promoters in the city's history and then spread the mania nationwide. A half million attendees a year now materialize at their meetings, which in 1996 will celebrate the thirtieth anniversary of the original NBC series.

The conclaves in Dearborn draw from across the Midwest. Usually there's a familiar face to trekkies, a celebrity from one of the Trek incarnations to answer questions and sign autographs. At concession booths in the building, you can buy just about every piece of Star Trek paraphernalia imaginable, from complete uniforms to face makeup (for perfecting that spiny Klingon forehead) to Mr. Spock's famous pointy ears. Other items up for sale to confirmed trekkies include license plate holders, bumper stickers, posters, toys, and other collectibles, from models and banks to books and underwear. But watch out. You might get hooked and find yourself beamed up into an autograph line. Like an epidemic from the planet Regula 7, Star Trek fever is highly contagious. For more information, call (313) 943–2350. To reach the Dearborn Civic Center, exit off the Southfield Freeway (Michigan 39) at Michigan Avenue and head 1 mile east to the signs.

Detroit

etroit. In World War II, when President Franklin D. Roosevelt referred to the "Arsenal of Democracy," he was talking about the Motor City. If you believe all you see on the nightly news, you'd think Detroit might have few things to offer the traveling family, but if you look closer, you'll find the city that's been slammed so much is on the way back and actually has so many activities to offer families that it deserves its own chapter here. There's something to do all year long in the city that still rightly claims its title as the world's automotive capital, from feeding deer while race cars compete nearby on the grounds of an urban park to visiting the world's largest museum devoted to the African American experience, scheduled to open in spring 1996. Leave your preconceived notions behind and see what the city offers. You'll be surprised.

BELLE ISLE ATTRACTIONS

Did you know that Michigan's largest city also is the setting for the nation's largest urban park? Once known as Hog Island because of the porkers placed there to rid the island of snakes, **Belle Isle** is Detroit's downtown playground, home to its own herd of deer, within sight of the state's tallest buildings.

On the 985-acre island in the middle of the Detroit River are so many family attractions, you couldn't do justice to them in an entire summer. Many of the activities are within walking distance of one another. Just park your car along one of the tree-lined boulevards and enjoy. The island is reached by exiting Interstate 75 at Jefferson Avenue and heading east. Turn right and cross onto the island at the Belle Isle Bridge.

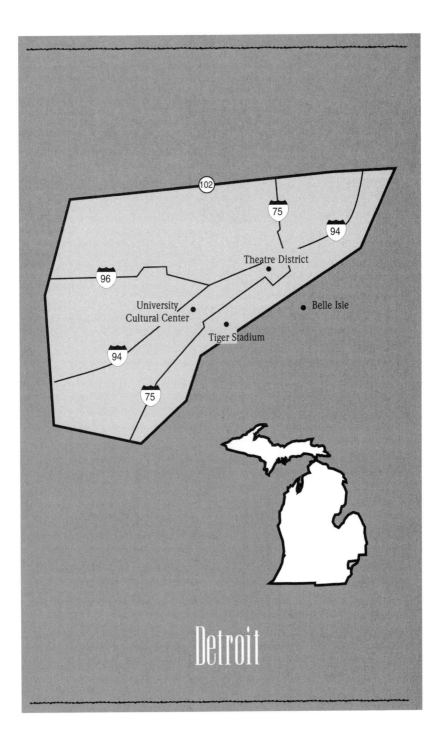

102

75

94

96

Theatre District

University
Cultural Center

Belle Isle

Tiger Stadium

94

75

Detroit

Outdoors, the **Belle Isle Zoo** was recently expanded from three to thirteen acres and now offers an African theme, with a rare opportunity for kids to get a look at wild animals from above along a ¾-mile-long elevated boardwalk. They'll see such creatures as two Sumatran tigers, three African lions, and a dozen wild turkeys among the twenty-one exhibits. The youngest children aren't forgotten, as there are domestic farm animals to pet and a fascinating "World of Spiders" where the kids can pit their squeamishness thresholds against one another. At the nearby **Belle Isle Nature Center,** there's a hospital where injured wild birds and other animals are brought by city residents to heal. Outside the zoo, the park is its own nature center, actually supporting upward of 120 European deer on the island's wooded interior. You'll often see some of the herd along the inner routes.

Indoors, the ninety-one-year-old **Belle Isle Aquarium**—the nation's oldest freshwater public aquarium—displays more than a hundred types of fish found in Michigan's lakes and streams or imported from around the world. Among the highlights are a freshwater stingray and an electric-eel exhibit that draws kids like a magnet. The zoo is open daily from May through October. Admission is a bargain at $1.00 for seniors over age sixty-two, 50 cents for children ages two through twelve, and $2.00 for others; call (313) 267–7159 for current information.

Surrounded by grounds from which you can see giant oceangoing and lake freighters pass by in the Detroit River, the **Whitcomb Conservatory** houses a unique display. It's a great place to explore the world of plants, from dessert settings for cacti to tropical humidity for ferns, palms, and banana trees. The conservatory's annual winter orchid and mum shows, two of six special events mounted here annually, are spectacular. Call (313) 267–7134 for details.

The **Dossin Great Lakes Museum** is a city treasure. While the marine radio crackles with the sounds of river traffic, kids can stand in the working wheelhouse of a former Great Lakes ore carrier. Marvel at the Gothic Room, with more than seven and a half tons of hand-carved oak work taken from a 1912 Great Lakes steamer, and see the first boat to break the 100-miles-per-hour barrier on a closed course. The museum is open Wednesday through Sunday from 10:00 A.M. to 5:00 P.M. and admission is by donation; call (313) 267–6440 for updates.

At the island's south end is **Scott Memorial Fountain,** a beautiful array of lights and spraying water during warm weather. If you've brought your swimsuit, there's even a public beach on the island's west side.

Every year in June, the island is taken over by race mania—both on land and on water. For the water race the fun shifts to the stretch of the river

**BILL'S TOP FAMILY ADVENTURES
IN DETROIT**

1. Museum of African-American History, downtown
2. Belle Isle Park, Detroit River
3. Detroit's Coney Islands, Lafayette Avenue
4. Detroit Cultural Center, Wayne State University Campus

between the island and the city, where the river's tricky currents are tested by up to a dozen Unlimited-class hydroplanes during the **Spirit of Detroit Thunderfest.** Two classes of boats actually compete over the four days, Unlimiteds and Grand Prix hydroplanes.

Now, for anyone who's never seen one of the Unlimiteds, we're talking serious boats here. This is powerboat racing's premier event, its version of the Kentucky Derby and the Indy 500. An estimated 400,000 fans come down to watch these boats, turning the event into a giant picnic beside the water. While others pay for grandstand seats, the majority either pick out a spot on the mainland or head to Belle Isle and watch for free (because of the heavy attendance, plan to get there early for a good spot). For a real treat take the kids during the time trials and buy them a pit pass for about $20, so they can see the boats, crews, and drivers up close. They have probably never seen anything like these speedy watercraft. With tall rear tails and race car–like fins to create downforce and keep the stern in the water, they're built to skip across the river surface with a high-pitched whine, shooting giant columns of water called "rooster tails" into the sky.

Mind you, this is a serious course. The huge Unlimited boats, powered by 3,000-horsepower turbines or World War II piston aircraft engines, roar over the water, tackling the wave troughs that develop as the water slaps the seawalls along Belle Isle—hurdles that rattle many a driver to the core. During the race, drivers encapsulated in enclosed cockpits like jet fighter pilots compete in several heats around a 2½-mile modified oval, running up to 225 miles per hour in the straights, slowing as they round the wider turn just upstream of the Belle Isle Bridge and again at the hairpin turn at the north end of the course. Boats compete on both Saturday and Sunday, with qualifying heats starting at 11:00 A.M. Top finishers rack up race points, and those with the highest totals earn a spot in the championship heat. Smaller, Grand Prix–class boats powered by automobile engines take to a shorter course at the same site, in between the big craft, but they're nothing to be ignored either, running at up to 150 miles per hour.

Since the noise can be very loud depending on where you sit, it's wise to wear earplugs (especially younger family members). Grandstand tickets range from about $2.00 to $125.00. For information call (313) 259–7760.

Only a week later the racing world again focuses on Belle Isle as the best Indianapolis-style race car drivers from the United States and Europe converge on its twisty track to see who can best the others during the **ITT Detroit Grand Prix.** Moved here from downtown a few years ago, the track has become a driver's favorite because it is so demanding.

Following days of practice and qualifying, the grounds around the track come alive on race day as more than 170,000 spectators jam onto the island, arriving by foot, by bus, or by shuttle from downtown restaurants (the MacArthur Bridge is closed to regular auto traffic). Millions more watch on television as these 900-horsepower, turbocharged cars make the run for the roses. The cars may sound like a pack of angry bees when they're on another part of the track, but when they go past your station, you'd better cover your children's ears or come equipped with earplugs. To say they're loud is an understatement. The race lasts two hours and fifteen minutes or 145 laps, whichever comes first.

Best vantage points around the track are in the grandstands, placed where the cars go under special pedestrian bridges and around the southern end of the island, past Scott Memorial Fountain, the Casino (actually a former dance pavilion), and down the main straight past the pits. General admission actually buys you just a place to stand and try to peer over the guardrails. Be prepared to balance your kids on your shoulders to let them see. If you're really lucky, you'll know someone who'll get you into one of the corporate tents, where, besides a great view from your own private grandstand, you can munch on lunch, which includes brownies first made by the wife of one of the drivers and now a tradition on the Indy car circuit.

After the Grand Prix is run, the fun isn't over, as cars with smaller engines also run the course. For ticket information call (800) DETROIT or (313) 393–7749.

STREET FESTIVALS

These annual racing events are just the prelude to two weeks of festivities that celebrate the world's longest peaceful international border in terms of length and years, during the **Detroit-Windsor International Freedom Festival.** Running from mid-June through July 4 each year, the activities reach a climax the week before U.S. Independence Day, when more than 10,000 fireworks blast off from three barges in the Detroit River during the **Hudson's International Freedom Festival Fireworks.** Bar none, this is the biggest family event of the year in downtown Detroit and Windsor (the Canadian city across the Detroit River) and it is said to be the largest pyrotechnic display in North America.

On fireworks day families begin gathering downtown in early afternoon. Mothers and fathers meet up after work or take the day off to spread picnic blankets on lawns across from Hart Plaza and elsewhere. As dusk settles in, commercial traffic on the Detroit River is halted and the swelling crowds, now numbering more than one million, excitedly line the streets and waterfronts of both Detroit and Windsor to watch the thirty-minute spectacle. At around 9:55 P.M. it starts. Shells up to 18 inches in diameter—that's bigger than those fired by the mightiest battleships during World War II—are launched high into the darkness, lighting up the sky over the river in a brilliant show that's fully choreographed to music and that can be seen and heard for miles up- and downstream.

Some of the best viewing spots might in fact be miles from the barges—first, because the more remote vantage points afford much quicker getaways if you have young ones to rush back home and, second, because you can share a toast with friends while you enjoy the fireworks' full effects. No alcohol is allowed on the plaza on fireworks day.

Other Freedom Festival activities include taking the kids to Canada—possibly their first visit to a foreign country—via the Ambassador Bridge or the Detroit-Windsor Tunnel. They can enjoy the carnival in downtown Windsor, other festival activities, or a meal at a sidewalk restaurant. They'll also enjoy the excitement on July 1, Canada Day, that country's version of our July 4. Windsor celebrates with what's billed as Canada's largest parade, plus crazy antics like the Great Bed Race downtown.

On the U.S. side a children's carnival and food fair in front of Ford Auditorium, the annual tugboat race on the river, and daily events on Hart Plaza, ranging from an international tug-of-war across the river against a team in Windsor to concerts for teens, lead up to the fireworks. For Freedom Fest information call (313) 923–7400.

During the festival and every weekend through Labor Day, you can let the kids pour on the hot sauce over authentic Mexican fare and test their palates, find a toy among the crafts makers, or join in the folk dancing demonstrations during the **Mexicantown Mercado.** On Sundays from 1:00 to 4:00 P.M., planners stage an array of family activities at Plaza Fiesta, located at the corner of Bagley and Twenty-first Street, the heart of the community. Children's pastimes include petting miniature goats, horses, and even cows. There are pony rides every weekend and kids can also learn traditional Hispanic games. Have them join in on the fun when one of the children, blindfolded, finally breaks a holiday piñata, scattering candy and chewing gum all over for the rest to gather in a headlong rush of sneakers and hands. Meanwhile, you can enjoy live music, check out cooking demonstrations given by famous Mexican-cook-book authors or chefs from the local restaurants (who explain how to can those hot chiles from the garden safely), or chat with Latin American artisans selling their crafts for adults and giving demonstrations on topics from tapestry mak-ing to Peruvian *retablo* (a handcrafted wooden box with two doors that usual-ly contains a scene from Indian life or a religious theme made from papier mâché. And don't forget the great restaurants for inexpensive Latin fare that's as mild or wild as you wish. To reach Mexicantown, exit Interstate 75 south-bound at Porter Street or northbound at Lafayette. Turn west and look for the banners along Bagley. For information call (313) 842–0450.

TOUR AND TASTE TIPS

Ever wonder how your morning or afternoon newspaper gets to your front porch every day? You can watch as one of the two metropolitan dailies pro-duced in downtown Detroit rolls off the presses if you visit the **Detroit News and Free Press.**

First head downtown to see how the stories and ads that appear in the paper each day travel from the imaginations of those who create them to your home. On Tuesday and Wednesday each week, you can take a ninety-minute tour of the editorial and advertising offices of the *News* and the *Free Press*—a great, educational first visit for children to a "real work world" environment.

Guides will take you to work areas on three floors of the *News* building, including the newsroom, where a reporter or editor, if not too busy working on that day's paper, explains how the journalists gather information for their sto-ries while out covering their "beats" and then return to their usually cluttered desks in the newsroom to write, using computers instead of typewriters.

The stories are then checked by editors, who decide where each piece will go in the next edition and what pictures will accompany them. The news-room may be busiest in the afternoons, but a morning visit is still enough for young minds to get a taste of the tension and excitement that fills the room come deadline time.

After visiting the display advertising area, where colorful ads are created for everything from stereos to washing machines, the group heads into the electronic composing room, where more computers turn the ads, artwork, and reporters stories into final graphic form and send them to the printing plant in Sterling Heights north of Detroit. Tours also are available of that facility, where rolls of paper weighing more than a ton each constantly feed into giant press-es, creating the finished product.

Tours are by reservation and begin at 9:30 A.M. at the *News* building, 615 West Lafayette, before moving to the *Free Press* at 321 West Lafayette. To reach the offices of the *News,* exit the southbound Lodge Freeway (Michigan 10) at Howard Street, continue one block to Lafayette, and turn right. To schedule a tour call (313) 223–4722 or (313) 222–6400.

Cincinnati may have its chili fries and New Orleans its Cajun jambalaya, but if you're looking for *the* authentic taste of Detroit either before or after a Red Wings game at Joe Louis Arena or events like the fireworks, there's no better place to experience it than the spot where the first hot dog was mated with bun and chili to become what's now known nationwide as a "Coney Island dog." It's been imitated by others, but if you're in the Motor City, the **Lafayette** and **American Coney Islands,** one snug against the other, are the places to try 'em.

Since 1918 both eateries, coincidentally begun by members of the same family, have served millions of tube steaks in a bun, slathered in a meaty chili that's just spicy enough, then layered with onions and topped with mustard that's deftly applied by the grill man with a wooden spoon. It's been that way

Don't pass up a chance to try a "Coney Island dog" at the Lafayette and American Coney Islands.

for generations of Detroiters who've pounded down Coneys accompanied by orange soda or other pop (the American also serves beer). You might be sitting next to a judge, a TV news anchor, or just a newspaper hawker. You'll meet the whole cross-section of the city.

Grab a seat and order a chili dog or two accompanied by a bowl of chili, or try something completely different, a Coney burger, loose ground beef in a bun and again, smothered in chili and onions. Then listen as the waiter sings out the song of the Coney: "Six on four, one no onions, four Cokes." Translation: two plates with two Coneys on each and two with one each. And these are real skin-on franks that pop when you bite into them. Those brave enough to risk a be-chilied shirt pick them up, while the more practical and the suit-and-tie crowd cut them with a fork.

Dessert? You'll probably have to go elsewhere, but even the kids won't mind. For long after you've left, they'll be savoring that great trio of aftertastes guaranteed to stay with them until they return with their own offspring. Don't worry. They'll invite you, too. Lafayette Coney Island is at 118 West Lafayette (313–964–8198) and the American is at 115 Michigan Avenue (313–961–7758). From the southbound Lodge Freeway (Michigan 10), exit at Howard Street, continue one block and turn left onto Lafayette. The restaurants are three blocks away, one block east of the U.S. courthouse. They're open daily, twenty-four hours a day.

THEATRICAL ADVENTURES

Just up the street from the Coney emporiums, along Woodward Avenue, a minirenaissance is taking place in what once was Detroit's glittering theater district. If you bring your family here just once for a movie or concert, their visit to the fabulously restored **Fox Theater** complex will stay with them the rest of their lives. It's the world's largest surviving 1920s movie palace.

From the gold-leafed lobby set off by magnificent simulated columns that evoke a scene from the movie *The Ten Commandments* (you expect to see Charlton Heston striding up to confront the Pharaoh any minute) to the huge, 5,000-seat auditorium with gargoyles and other characters staring down from everywhere under a tentlike dome, the Fox is a tribute to architect C. Howard Crane and those who rescued this beauty from sure ruin. Your kids will instantly recognize that this is no mall multiplex.

After opening in 1928 the theater fell on hard times in the 1970s. With its ornate features failing, it was saved by Little Caesar's Pizza king Mike Ilitch. Millions were spent on its restoration, and since it reopened in 1988 it's been a hit regardless of who plays there. Many in the audience, in fact, don't care who's on stage. They've come to marvel at the theater itself. Performers who've returned to the stage of the Fox include crooners like Tony Bennett—who's been rediscovered by the college set. Holiday children's shows also draw the crowds, as do big-screen movie epics shown each summer.

The Fox's success has led another theater, geared to youths, to open across the street. The **State Theater** presents everything from irreverent movies like the Monty Python comedy epics to local and nationally famous "grunge" rock groups. On other nights it turns into a young people's nightclub called **Club X.** Kids can take their first date to the fancy French restaurant **Tres Vite** at the Fox or to the art deco **Elwood Grill** for burgers. For a playbill of performers at either theater, call (313) 396–7600.

A few blocks to the south is a theater set aside just for kids from the wiggle set on up. From October through May the **Detroit Youtheater** presents weekend programs to introduce youngsters to all types of performing arts, at the 1,700-seat Music Hall Center.

There are two series of shows. The first, appropriately called the Wiggle Club, is for youngsters ages three to six. The Movin' Up Club is for kids age seven and above. Twelve different productions are presented each season, ranging from plays like *The Little Prince* to the return of Ishangi, the West African dance company that visits each February as part of Black History Month (the troupe has appeared for twenty-eight straight years!).

In about half of the productions, performers answer questions from the audience. The Youtheater also offers performance workshops that help young people learn the fundamentals of acting and dance. Theater tickets are $7.00 each and workshops are $8.00. The Music Hall Center, which completed the final phase of a total renovation in 1995, is at 350 Madison Avenue. To reach it take Interstate 75 and exit at Madison Avenue. The theater is a few blocks to the right. Call (313) 963–7622.

AUTO SHOWS

It's long been a January tradition in southeastern Michigan to shake off those postholiday doldrums with a trip downtown to one of two annual events at Cobo Center that pay homage to the product that made Detroit famous.

The largest automobile exhibition on the continent, the **North American International Auto Show** isn't just a stage for Detroit automakers alone to march out their new models. More than forty manufacturers from across the world now showcase more than seven hundred cars and trucks to the nearly 700,000 potential car buyers and the just plain curious who come to admire the conglomerations of glass, steel, and rubber.

Visiting this show is like entering the world's largest new-car showroom, as each maker hires dancers, singers, and models, and carts out glitzy rides that kids and grown-ups alike stand in line to try. Everywhere, kids walk by with bags full of advertising brochures and line up for a chance to sit behind the wheel of a new Mustang, Camaro, or other sporty model, while their parents check out the minivans.

Other showstoppers include the concept cars that are always introduced at this event, exhibits that show youngsters how auto engineers work to design next year's models, and drawings of concept cars done by local college and high-school students. On Cobo's lower level the kids will also be able to bounce on the sofa beds and try out the TVs in the latest van conversions or grab a snack at the concessions area.

To reach Cobo take the southbound Lodge Freeway (Michigan 10) downtown and follow the exit signs to rooftop or underground parking at the convention center. Parking is also available in street-level lots. Crowds can be heavy on weekends, so it might be wise to plan a weeknight visit. And because of the crowds and the excitement, be sure to keep track of your kids, or arrange to meet the older ones periodically at predetermined sites. For show information call (810) 643–0250.

Before Detroit's gala auto show went international, there was another, some would say even glitzier auto show, one featuring ingenious and sometimes downright outlandish cars every year. And each year, the annual **Autorama** custom car show at Cobo Center continues to live up to that reputation. Like the other big Detroit car show, there's no age group this production doesn't appeal to if you've got a "caroholic" family member or two.

Everyone from preteens to grown-ups will marvel at seeing favorite custom cars that have appeared in national auto magazines. Lacquered hot rods with gleaming chrome engines, side pipes, and wheels—pinstriped beauties that run the gamut from 1934 Fords and 1969 Corvettes to modified Mercedes—are polished and awaiting the car aficionado's review. Up to 500 custom models cover the display floor at Cobo.

Most of the entries are the pride and joy of average shade-tree mechanics who've worked on the cars in their own garages for a chance at showing them off. The show also features special exhibits, such as a display of nearly a hundred Harley-Davidson motorcycles and specialty cars from recent movies.

Along with the stars of steel, stars of sports and television are present to sign autographs. Past appearances have included nationally known soap opera stars and sports celebrities such as Detroit Tigers slugger Cecil Fielder signing autographs for the kids, and even "Buffalo Bob" Smith and Howdy Doody doing the same for baby boomers. Best of all, with your admission comes the chance to pick out a favorite car and vote for it as best of the show. Other judges award trophies to winners in each class. For information on dates and ticket prices, call (810) 650–5566 or (810) 650–5560.

CULTURAL CENTER ATTRACTIONS

The antique cars, the Conestoga wagon, the model-train exhibit, and the fascinating "Streets of Old Detroit" are just a few of the highlights of a visit to the **Detroit Historical Museum,** part of the complex of buildings near Wayne State University called the University Cultural Center. The museum's focus on the city's past and future is made especially appealing for youngsters, who have fun while exploring the city's history at the same time.

The museum's trademark is on the lower level. In a darkened streetscape lit by "streetlamps," visitors walk the cobbled streets of a mock-up of what the city looked like in the 1800s, before the automobile transformed it forever. You can peer into the homes and businesses, almost expecting the mannequins to come alive as they sit pictured counting out the day's receipts or making purchases. Other museum favorites include a 15-by-25-foot miniature-train layout run by sensors. Just step up to the exhibit and the system comes to life. The layout changes regularly and may depict a small-town scene, circus trains, even a rodeo coming to town.

A new exhibit on the first floor is "The Motor City," an interactive display that includes a 70-foot section of the assembly line of a former General Motors Detroit Cadillac assembly plant, with an operating "body drop," where the body of a car is slid onto the chassis. Also included is an exhibit where kids can actually crank and start a replica Model T Ford. At "Furs to Factories, Detroit at Work from 1701 to 1901," they can see the development of the city from a French fur-trading post to the world's car capital. The museum is at 5401 Woodward Avenue at Kirby. It and the other Cultural Center attractions highlighted here are reached by exiting Interstate 94 at Woodward Avenue/John R and heading south on either John R or Woodward about half a mile to Kirby. From Interstate 75, exit at Warren Avenue and head west to Woodward; then go two blocks north. Parking is in a lot behind the museum off Kirby. Admission is by donation. For more information call (313) 833–1805.

Kitty-corner from the historical museum is one of the largest publicly owned art museums in the nation, the **Detroit Institute of Arts.** Now before the kids wrinkle their noses up at the uncool thought of going to an art museum, tell them to be patient. This one is different.

While many museum employees gulp when they see kids coming, the DIA has plenty of exhibits that invite youngsters to touch and explore on their

ANNUAL EVENTS FOR THE FAMILY IN DETROIT

North American International Auto Show, mid-January, Cobo
Center, (810) 643–0250

Detroit Boat Show, early February, Cobo Center, (810) 877–8240

Spirit of Detroit Thunderfest/APBA Gold Cup, early June, Detroit
River, (313) 259–7760

ITT Detroit Grand Prix, mid-June, Belle Isle Race Course,
(313) 393–7749 or (800) DETROIT

International Freedom Festival, late June, downtown,
(313) 932–7400

Michigan State Fair, late August through Labor Day, fairgrounds,
(313) 368–1000

Michigan Thanksgiving Day Parade, Woodward Avenue
downtown, (313) 923–7400

own and that start them on the road to appreciating art in all its forms.

There are several sure-bet draws for kids inside, says William H. Peck, curator of ancient art at the DIA: armor, mummies, the spiral staircase, the American house, the "donkey," and a special treasure hunt game, "The Mystery of the Five Fragments." The game motivates young visitors to discover the museum and its art with enthusiasm, overcoming any reluctance by sending them throughout the galleries in search of clues to solve the mystery.

The donkey, by artist Rene Sintas, welcomes kids to climb, hang, and otherwise play all over it till their energy's spent. The most popular exhibit for kids, however, is the display of ancient Egyptian art and artifacts. Included is a beautifully preserved gilded, masked mummy. They'll learn that underneath is the body of a woman dating from the Roman occupation, around the first or second century A.D. X rays show she was in her thirties or forties and that at her death and she apparently had no physical deformities. She's now in a display case with four jars the Egyptians once used—get this, kids—to store the mummy's internal organs.

In the recently renovated Great Hall, museum goers can see up to a dozen suits of armor dating from the thirteenth to the eighteenth century, now lit by fiber optics to highlight the craftsmanship, while another case features swords, daggers, and other edge weapons. At the American house kids can explore a reconstructed portion of a Philadelphia residence called Whitby Hall. The spiral staircase is not historically significant, according to curator Peck. Designers just used it to tie the Gothic period on the floor above to the Romanesque-period floor below, and it's turned into a convenient kid shortcut and imagination enhancer. For information on children's programs and hours, call (313) 833–7900.

After you finish exploring the DIA, walk behind the building and visit the colorful **Detroit Science Center,** which offers fun for everyone from toddlers on up. One of the highlights is taking a seat before the 3½- story-high Omnimax Theater screen, reached after traveling through a rainbow of neon colors on the 80-foot-long escalator tunnel. Then, on the huge domed screen, lights dim as sixteen loudspeakers erupt and you are taken on a seat-of-the-pants flight aboard the space shuttle, on a flight skimming over a canyon frothing with white water, on a jungle trek into the rain forest, or on some other spectacular film excursion. You'll leave awed but ready for the next adventure, just down the hall.

This is school science made fun. In a demonstration of static electricity, kids touch a generator and their hair stands on end. See a laser display and other live science experiments in the Discovery Theater area, among the more than fifty hands-on exhibits. Smaller children love the "Magic Schoolbus Corner," patterned after a popular television show, where touch-screen computers introduce them to the world of science. The Science Center is at 5020 John R at Warren. From Interstate 75, exit at Warren and go west to Brush. Turn right, then go left. The center is open from 10:00 A.M. to 2:00 P.M. on weekdays and from 10:30 A.M. to 6:00 P.M. on weekends; Omnimax shows are presented hourly. Admission of $6.50 for teens and adults and $4.50 for children ages four through twelve includes the theater and all demonstrations. Parking is available in the adjacent lot for $3.00. For more information call (313) 577–8400.

Also close by, at 301 Frederick Douglass and John R, is the **Museum of African-American History.** The present building opened in 1987, the realized dream of Detroit physician Charles Wright, who thought black children needed to remember the story of their ancestors. The museum grew from a small exhibit in his home to the present building. In 1996 the museum will move once again, to new quarters nearby that will be four times larger than the present building. It will be the world's largest facility devoted to the African

American experience and will feature some of the most extensive interactive exhibits of any museum in the nation.

Detroit's African American roots run deep, and visitors' introductory image will be the site of a nearly full-scale replica slave ship. On its surface will appear 7,000 names of ships that carried Africans across the Atlantic to the Americas.

Children can push a button on a time line of video screens and learn about African life before the slave trade and how slaves were placed on the auction block if they survived the crossing. The exhibit traces the diverse history of African Americans to the present day, including an entry about Benjamin Franklin, the first African American space shuttle astronaut. Visitors will also learn about the Underground Railroad, the series of safe houses through which escaped slaves fled the South to freedom in the North before the Civil War. The network had many so-called stations, and one of its most active terminals was Detroit, where the refugees were transported across the Detroit River into Canada.

This will also be the first time Detroit's role in the African American experience and in national and international history will be highlighted at the museum, including little-known facts such as how John Brown and Frederick Douglass held secret meetings in the city shortly before Brown's famous raid on Harpers Ferry, West Viriginia, before the Civil War. Little-recognized inventors such as Garrett Morgan, the Detroit man who developed the first working traffic light, will also be featured.

During the holidays there's always a special presentation on Kwanza. Swahili for "first fruits," the traditional celebration is based on the harvest, which occurs in many African countries during December. Teaching principles to live by as well as offering a chance to celebrate, Kwanza reaffirms a commitment to seven strong moral ideals, including a belief in self and the importance of the family. A significant amount of the museum's four exhibit areas will be dedicated to educating not only children but adults as well. The new building also includes a restaurant. The enlarged museum is scheduled to open in winter of 1997 at the corner of Warren Avenue and Brush Street in the Cultural Center, adjacent to the Children's Museum and the Detroit Institute of Arts. To reach the museum, exit Interstate 75 at Warren and go west to Brush, or from Interstate 94, exit at Woodward Avenue/John R and take John R south. For information about admission costs and hours of operation, call (313) 833–9800.

Just a block away, at 67 East Kirby, across the street from the Detroit Institute of Arts north wing, is the **Detroit Children's Museum.** Run by the city's public schools, the museum is open to the public from noon to 4:00 P.M. Saturdays and during special events such as the Freedom Festival. The museum is mainly keyed to allow the younger crowd to take their imaginations to the limit. A visit here is a good accompaniment either before or after exploring the Detroit Science Center, a block away.

On Saturdays there are two free shows in the museum's thirty-two-seat planetarium geared to children and parents who may not be familiar with the night sky. The museum is one of the focal points during Detroit's annual Freedom Festival Children's Day. Kids can try their hand at painting at easels set up outside, along with face painting, creating silk-screened T-shirts, and other activities.

Permanent exhibits like a full-size example of an Asian tiger teach children about animals, while others focus on cultures as varied as those of the Inuit Eskimos and the peoples of Indonesia and Africa. Toddlers will find plenty of fun in the Children's Discovery Room, where they can test their skills with blocks and other toys that also teach. Be sure to ask for the treasure hunt game (similar to the DIA's) that takes kids on discovery safari through the building. In the museum's art gallery, the work of some of Detroit's best artists are on display in a collage depicting the city's African American heritage since the 1950s, and its industrial heritage is represented by the museum mascot–a horse fashioned from 900 pounds of chrome auto bumpers on the museum's front lawn. For program information call (313) 494–1210.

You can combine a visit to all the above attractions and take in an art fair at the same time during September's **Detroit Festival of Arts.** This annual celebration attracts more than 250,000 fair goers and more than 125 artists and craftspeople from across the country.

Three main stages feature nearly nonstop blues, gospel, jazz, and rhythm-and-blues music and other activities, as all streets in the fifteen-block area around the Cultural Center and Wayne State University are closed to auto traffic. A major component of the fest is the huge children's fair, with more than seventy groups providing activities and educational experiences. At IBM's children's fair, for example, kids can try their hands on a computer.

A literary-arts program features poetry reading just for youngsters, and in Wayne State's DeRoy Auditorium, there are continuous film screenings, including a Sunday-afternoon block of shows produced for–and, in some cases, by— youngsters. A recycling demonstration teaches how to make recycled paper and how someone's trash becomes someone else's treasure through reuse. Other programs just for fun feature fire eaters, tightrope walkers, children's song performers, and puppeteers. Lots of "make and take" crafts activities are included, too.

For teens and parents, more than fifty performers entertain on the main stages. At various times you might see a New Orleans break-dancer or someone playing the spoons, while at another spot you can clog to bluegrass or limbo to the beat of a Haitian steel drum. In between, shop for a painting, basket, or item of handmade clothing among the artists' booths. And don't forget the food stalls. For more information call (313) 577–5088.

HOLIDAY TRADITIONS AND OTHER PASTIMES

Two months later you can attend an annual event that children of all ages look forward to—not just in metro Detroit, but across the country: the annual **Michigan Thanksgiving Day Parade.** Televised nationwide, the nearly seventy-year-old event signals the traditional kickoff to the holidays. The excitement of floats, marching bands, and balloons amid the city skyscrapers on a crisp November morning—and finally, the sight every child waits for, Santa's sleigh—is all here.

Featuring nearly 100 units, including 25 floats, 21 bands, and 14 giant balloons, the event draws an estimated 1.1 million viewers along the parade route. The fun starts at 9:15 A.M. at Woodward and Mack, near the Cultural Center. The parade then heads downtown on Woodward, to Hart Plaza at Jefferson Avenue.

Along with old favorite floats that spectators never tire of, the parade also includes at least one balloon and one float based on winning designs submitted by local elementary-school students. For the best view buy a grandstand seat. Or get there early—by 6:00 A.M. for the 9:00 A.M. parade start—to watch at streetside. The final float, of course, is Santa himself, who gets the key to the hearts of Michigan children. For information call (313) 923–7400.

In conjunction with the holiday festivities, the Cobo Center hosts the annual **Christmas Carnival,** featuring a chance for kids to visit Santa and Mrs. Claus and to romp in an indoor amusement park with Ferris wheel, carousels, and other rides you'd expect to find here only in summer. Christmas Carnival admission is free, but the amusement ride tickets are separate. Call (313) 877–8111 for details.

Want a museum with a different beat? Check out one of Michael Jackson's famed sequined gloves and the cramped studio where the likes of Diana Ross, the Temptations, Marvin Gaye, the Four Tops, and Stevie Wonder put Detroit on the world's music map, at the **Motown Historical Museum.** In two side-by-side homes, composer and producer Berry Gordy lived and produced hits for those and scores of other performers from Detroit's neighborhoods who went on to recording glory in the studios he named "Hitsville, USA." With Motown hits playing in the background, guided, handicapped-accessible tours lead past the gift shop and other rooms where the raw talent

Gordy discovered was refined to the point that it eventually performed in front of heads of state worldwide.

You'll also get a chance to see the tiny garage-turned-studio where musicians and singers crammed themselves in to create records that sold millions worldwide, and you'll hear a "recording session" in progress, with the sounds of musicians, singers, and engineers composing a Motown hit. Upstairs, the apartment where Gordy and his family lived includes the kitchen table that served as his office, looking as if he'd just left it. Other displays help tell the history of the company through wall-size photos.

In conjunction with the museum, hop aboard the Attractions Shuttle (running May through August) or drive twenty minutes to Dearborn's Henry Ford Museum (see page 18) for its joint exhibit on the Motown sound, which sponsors hope will eventually be on permanent display at the Motown Museum. Walk along the "Road to Motown," where visitors look through porthole-shaped openings—including some just high enough for children—to test their record knowledge.

A hands-on exhibit lets kids try their hand at creating a record or introducing a hit as a radio disc jockey. They can even follow a video to learn a few of the dance moves that made the Temptations famous. In a nightclub setting watch an eighteen-minute video history of Motown that includes the artists and Gordy discussing the impact of the city on their music and the impact of their music on the world. Then follow the Motown sound through the years by walking through a hall where on one side highlights each song that made the charts and its artist the other side recalls a moment in history when those songs were hits.

Admission to the Motown Historical Museum is $6.00 adults, $5.00 for seniors ages sixty and over, $4.00 for students twelve to eighteen, and $3.00 for children eleven and under. From the Lodge Freeway (Michigan 10), exit at the Milwaukee/West Grand Boulevard exit and head east on Grand Boulevard. The museum is at 2648 West Grand, on the south side; call (313) 875–2264 for more information. The Henry Ford Museum portion of the exhibit is included with that museum's admission charge. To reach the Ford Museum from Motown, take the Lodge Freeway south to Interstate 94 westbound and go 12 miles to the Oakwood Boulevard exit. Follow Oakwood north and turn right onto Village Road. Call (313) 271–1620 for other details.

What can be more natural than taking the family out to the ball game? **Tiger Stadium**—the home of Detroit Tiger greats Al Kaline, Ty Cobb, Hank Greenberg, and Willie Horton—invites you to see the major-league boys of summer and root the "Tigs" on to a repeat of their most recent World Series wins, in 1968 and 1984.

Who wouldn't have a great time spending the afternoOn at Tiger Stadium? (Courtesy Detroit Tigers)

Team owner and Little Caesar's Pizza big cheese Mike Ilitch may be debating the pros and cons of a new stadium with state politicos, but for now venerable Tiger Stadium, built in 1912, is home to the club for at least a few more years. From opening day in early April to the last game in the fall, the 52,000-seat stadium is a magical place where the smells of steamed hot dogs and peanuts mix with the crack of the bat and the roar—or boos—of the crowd. Tiger Stadium underwent positive changes when Ilitch bought the team a few years ago. Now when they step inside the gates, most fans first head for the food court called Tiger Plaza, which has a lot more choices than just hot dogs. Chew on a slice of pizza, enjoy a burger, or sample Mexican food while searching for a game souvenir at one of the concession booths.

Other special family incentives include the Kid's Row game area behind the grandstand seats on the concourse and promotional days throughout the year, including cap, ball, and glove days, when youngsters get free Tigers gear. Also watch for more unusual promotions, like free-beach-towel or free-back-pack days.

Paws, the Tiger mascot, who is usually found roaming the food court before the game, head into the stands during play to cheer on the home team; and, of course, everybody joins in singing "Take Me Out to the Ball Game" during the seventh-inning stretch. One popular attraction happens after every Monday game. Kids can line up along the first-base side and, at least once in their lives, play big leaguer by running the bases. Tiger Stadium is at the corner of Michigan Avenue (U.S. 12) and Trumbull. From Interstate 94 take either Michigan Avenue east or Trumbull and follow the signs to parking around the stadium. For game schedules call (313) 962–4000.

It's the amazement at hearing the throaty blasts of a nearly seventy-year-old theater organ introducing a Laurel-and-Hardy comedy classic. It's watching Humphrey Bogart in *Casablanca* or *The African Queen* on the big screen, or the spectacle of *Lawrence of Arabia*. It's blithely "nyucking" along with the crowd at the antics of the Three Stooges. Enjoying classic movies in an old-time, neighborhood theater setting is a practice that's still alive and well at the historic **Redford Theater.**

The Redford caters to families with its series of G-rated and ageless flicks. You owe it to your kids to introduce them to the experience of seeing movies on the big screen instead of the puny alternatives offered by the home video player or the local multiplex. In fact, the Redford's owners, the Motor City Theater Organ Society, say the Redford has become a haven for dating teens and parents with children.

The Redford shows movies to the public on alternate weekends. Other times, it's open to society members for theater organ concerts. Designed in an Oriental motif, the interior features giant warriors and other figures towering over its 1,500 seats (which include some that are handicapped accessible). All-volunteer crews recently restored the inner lobby, scrubbing off old paint and replacing two chandeliers, and also restored the auditorium ceiling, which now gleams with starlike lights fixed in a blue background.

Before each feature, the kids will get a kick out of encountering something they—and possibly you—have never experienced: a thirty-minute concert performed on the giant 800-pipe, ten-rank Barton Golden Voice theater organ that can imitate everything from a tuba to a classical orchestra.

Among the attractions at the Redford are Laurel-and-Hardy and Three Stooges festivals and a special viewing of the Buster Keaton film classic *Steamboat Bill Jr.* Movie tickets are a steal at just $2.50 each; and occasional special shows range from $8.00 to $15.00. Theater tours also are available. The Redford Theater is at 17360 Lahser Road, between Grand River Avenue and Seven Mile Road in Detroit. To reach it exit the Southfield Freeway (Michigan 39) at Grand River and turn west to Lahser, then head north. Call (313) 537–2560 for a recorded schedule.

Detroit Northeast

T his region of southeastern Michigan skirts metropolitan Detroit's northern suburbs, taking in parts of western Livingston, eastern Wayne, and Oakland, Macomb, and St. Clair counties, at the base of Michigan's Thumb. In summer this is the region's "concert central," home of outdoor venues that bring in some of music's greatest stars. In contrast, though, it also offers visits to the baronial mansions of auto pioneers, as well as beautiful beaches and parks that entertain families all year round.

FARMINGTON HILLS

Marvin's Marvelous Mechanical Museum is a great name for one of the most interesting and peculiar collections of things that whir, click, toot, and tick that you will ever see. Started by Marvin Yagoda, a pharmacist with a definite fascination for things mechanical, the museum is filled with seemingly every coin-operated nickelodeon or other carnival coin-swallowing machine that's ever been made. See what your future holds according to Madame Zelda, a 1917 fortune-telling machine, or bat against the baseball players of yesteryear in a 1937 World Series game. There's even one from England's Brighton Pier featuring a metallic Spanish Inquisition.

Among the more than 250 mechanical devices dating from the late 1850s are "kiss-o-meters" that measure the power of your pucker, together with the latest laser hologram video games. The museum has become so popular since Yagoda opened it in 1990 that it's been a regular on television shows from the *Mickey Mouse Club* to national morning talk programs.

One "don't miss" attraction amid the 5,500 square feet of signs, clocks,

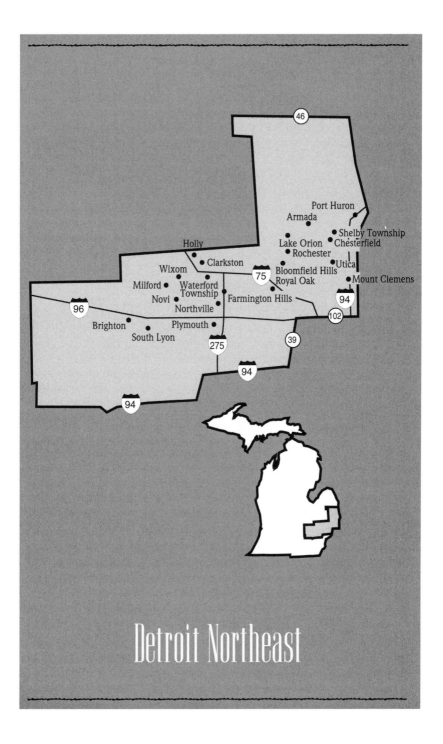

Detroit Northeast

flags, and other paraphernalia is what Yagoda feels is his most prized posses-
sion, a copy of Phineas T. Barnum's famed "Cardiff Giant," the bogus petrified
human that the nineteenth-century showman displayed to his customers—the
suckers who, as he was purportedly fond of saying, were born every minute.
Marvin's display is unlike any other in the world—one that would have made
old P. T. himself proud. Admission is free, but Yagoda's no fool. You'll have to
drop a quarter into each device to operate it. The museum is at 31005 West
Orchard Lake Road. To reach it take Orchard Lake Road north from Interstate
696. Turn left into the Hunter's Square shopping center at 14 Mile Road. Call
(810) 626–5020 for hours of operation.

PLYMOUTH

Imitated but never duplicated, the annual **Plymouth International Ice
Sculpture Spectacular** in mid-January draws more than 100,000 persons to
the streets of this normally placid colonial downtown to ogle hundreds of
sculptures carved from 400-pound blocks of ice. The event is one of the best
of its kind, as carvers come to chip, chop, smooth, grind, and buff their way
through town as they form more than 200 works of fleeting, crystalline art.

Ice carvers from as far as Japan and Russia compete in the professional
category, as one- or two-person teams go against one another. They each have
three hours to complete their entries, which are judged on originality and
detail. Their sculptures, up to eight feet high, are protected from the sun in a
downtown parking structure so the public can enjoy them longer, and the public can drive past them when they're done. But the big draw is in Kellogg Park
downtown, where more than a dozen huge figures weighing several tons take
shape.

A special walking path winds past ice statues and parents hold bundled
youngsters on their shoulders to view the works, which in years past have
included castles and dragons. The sculptures are especially impressive at night,
when they're bathed in brilliant colored lights. Adjacent to the main display, a
special exhibit for kids usually includes up to twenty fantasy ice sculptures, and
there's an annual Saturday fireworks show, too.

Smaller sculptures are also placed in front of many downtown stores,
which stay open for folks to come in, warm up, and, just perhaps, to make a
purchase. There's also food and hot drinks available from vendors in the park.
If you can't make the actual festival, don't worry. When the weather cooperates, many of the works stay in place until they disappear into a puddle in a
week or so.

To reach Plymouth follow Interstate 275 to Ann Arbor Road; then turn west and go about a mile and a half. Turn north on Main Street, find a parking spot, and follow the crowds downtown. For exact dates and more information, call (313) 459–6969.

NORTHVILLE

Got a budding child actor in the house? This might be his or her chance to break into the big time. For the last fifteen years, in a theater nearly a century old in quaint downtown Northville, the unique **Marquis Theater** has been producing drama that makes stars out of children.

Owner/producer Inge Zayti began the Marquis featuring adult actors but later found her niche introducing children to the stage. In addition to spending the summer working with would-be actors, she presents children's-oriented plays from March through December. Recent performances have included *The Princess and the Pea, Peter Pan,* and *Heidi,* all performed by children between eight and eighteen. In summer Zayti cultivates new talent by offering a two-week day camp that features acting and singing activities for kids who want to give the bright lights a whirl. She's assisted by five instructors. Zayti also plans to open a live-in children's summer theater camp.

Tickets are $5.00 for all-child performances and $6.50 for shows with children and adults. The Marquis is at 135 East Main. To find Northville, exit Interstate 275 at Eight Mile Road and head west; turn south at Center and then east at Main. The theater is on the right side; call (810) 349–8110.

There are plenty of other draws that this small downtown has for the entire family as well. At 302 East Main, for example, you can outfit the family with acoustic music instruments and lessons at the **GitFiddler,** which also cosponsors the annual **Northville Folk and Bluegrass Festival** to benefit Huntington's disease research. The festival is always the last Sunday in July at Ford Field, along Hutton/Dunlop Street, one block north of Main. The fest kicks off with an 11:00 A.M. pancake breakfast at the field. Admission is $10.00 in advance and $12.00 at the gate for teens and adults; $6.00 for seniors and for kids ages twelve and under. Infants are free. For information and tickets call the store at (810) 349–9420.

Be sure to drop by what might be the city's most popular bakery, the **Great Harvest Bread Company,** at 139 East Main. It specializes in great breads and in pastry combinations you've probably never imagined. Call (810) 344–4404 for the day's featured selection. Lots of other shops and restaurants downtown will keep you busy the entire day. If you've a mind to, take the family on a picnic at the start of **Middle Rouge Parkway,** nicknamed **Hines Park,** after the Edward N. Hines Parkway, which runs through it. The park is a 16-mile-long continuous greenbelt from Northville to Dearborn, following the Middle Rouge River valley. Picnic areas, swings, slides, and softball diamonds are everywhere and there are three man-made lakes (unfortunately, they are not open for swimming). To reach the park from downtown Northville, take Center south to the first light and turn east, then veer to the right.

NOVI

Attention, all followers of Superman, Superboy, Spawn, and other forces of good and evil lurking in the pages of that American pulp icon, the comic book. Here's a show that'll even warm Lex Luthor's heart.

The annual **Comic Con,** or comic-book convention, is an event where father, mother, son, and daughter are on equal footing if they're like the rest of the crowd here: eager to pore over the more than 120,000 square feet of comics and memorabilia assembled in Novi's Expo Center.

Comic publishers from DC to Schism are on hand to discuss with fans and collectors exactly what should or shouldn't befall their superhero in the next installment of the real pulp fiction. But don't scoff. These are serious buffs, who've been known to pay thousands for a rare premier issue of a particular superhero comic-book series.

Besides collectors looking to buy, sell, and trade, you'll find art contests geared to finding burgeoning illustrators who might already be creating the next superhero at home, charity auctions of comic art to benefit groups like the Muscular Dystrophy Association, and perhaps even a Red Cross blood drive on the premises. Comic-book experts lead discussions of the latest trends and artists autograph their work. And while Hollywood has its glitzy movie premieres, Comic Con has world premier showings of cartoons and, occasionally, even the debut of a new superhero.

If you are even the slightest bit interested in the world of comics or you think that it's finally time to trade in those volume-number-one issues of Donald Duck or Batman that you've been saving for your kid's college funds, this is the place to start the bidding.

To get to the Novi Expo Center, leave Interstate 96 at exit 162, Novi Road, and go south about one block. The center is at the southwest corner of the freeway interchange. If you can't make it to this version of Comic Con, which takes place in late March, there's another each October at Dearborn's Civic Center. Admission to the Novi show is $10 per person or about $25 for all three days; children under age five enter free. Call (810) 350–2633 for show hours and exact dates.

Novi might seem to the uninformed to be a strange place to have a "motorsports hall of fame," but not to those who've heard of the famed Novi Indianapolis cars. And the fact that Novi is on the outskirts of the Motor City just might have something to do with the location of this engine lovers' mecca.

The **Motorsports Hall of Fame of America** pays tribute to all sports that the automobile, internal-combustion-powered or otherwise, is connected to, whether on land or water. If you follow racing, a stop here is a must during any Detroit-area visit.

Challenge your companions to a run on the hall's four-lane slot car track, where scale model electric-motor stock cars held onto to the course by a pin inside a slot (hence the name) race around a track; or climb into the coin-operated video simulation car race that pits you against another driver.

The actual hall of fame now includes sixty-six inductees and features plaques honoring great drivers, mechanics, and others involved in all forms of motorsports. New names are added each year.

Inside the main exhibit area, changing displays include seventy racing vehicles—from current Indy-style cars, stock cars, and drag strip models to turn-of-the century vehicles, including motorcycles and powerboats. Also on display is the 1965 incarnation of the Novi special, an all-wheel-drive car driven at Indianapolis by Bobby Unser. The famed supercharged engine was built in Novi, and although it never completed the 500, it was always known as one of the most powerful racing engines that ever ran at the track.

You'll also see one of the famous Green Monster racers. Powered by a 17,500-horsepower jet engine, the car still holds the speed record for an open-cockpit car: 342 miles per hour. Another record holder on display is the Miss U.S. 1 Unlimited-class hydroplane, which ran a measured mile course at 200 miles per hour in 1960.

Kids can have their picture taken in the driver's seat of a real Winston Cup stock car—a treat they'll remember for a long time. Four video screens play race footage throughout the display area, while a gift shop supplies everything from die-cast model cars to T-shirts and other wearables, collector cards, videos, and more. The hall of fame is located at the Novi Expo Center (see directions above) and is open from 10:00 A.M. to 5:00 P.M. daily except major holidays. Admission costs $3.00 for seniors and children under twelve and $5.00 for others. Call (810) 349–7223 for more information.

ROYAL OAK

OK, so the **Detroit Zoological Park** is not really in Detroit but in this revitalized community at the city's northern edge. Wise planners placed the 125-acre

BILL'S TOP FAMILY ADVENTURES IN DETROIT NORTHEAST

1. Motorsports Hall of Fame of America, Novi
2. Detroit Zoological Park, Royal Oak
3. Huron–Clinton Metroparks, Milford
4. Mt. Brighton Skiing, Brighton
5. Pine Knob and Meadowbrook Summer Music Festivals, Pine Knob/Meadowbrook

park here in 1928, the first in the nation to use barless exhibits, place animals in settings as close to their natural environment as possible, and confine them using dry or water moats for an unobstructed view.

One of the zoo's most popular features isn't an animal at all. It's the Detroit Zoo Miniature Railroad, given to the zoo in 1931 by the *Detroit News*. Engines were donated by the Chrysler Corporation in the 1950s and renovated in 1982. The trains transport nearly half a million passengers 1¼ miles from the Main Station near the front gate, through a tunnel, to Africa Station, at the farthest corner of the park, and back again.

Many families begin their zoo visits by heading to the **Rackham Memorial Fountain** in the park's center. Its 10-foot-tall bronze bears surrounded by sculptures of turtles, frogs, and life-size sea lions make the 75,000-gallon fountain a great spot for pictures.

Live-animal exhibits show off the zoo's collection of nearly 3,000 creatures, from grizzly bears to tiny frogs. The bear dens are among the most popular attractions, with polar bears, grizzlies, and sloth bears lounging on the rocklike climbing areas or frolicking in their own pools to cool off in summer. Alligators, caimans, and crocodiles, along with an extensive collection of snakes, are housed in the **Holden Museum of Living Reptiles and Amphibians.** The whole family will enjoy the **Wilson Aviary Wing,** a large free-flight building with a waterfall and hundreds of live plants that create a jungle-like environment for more than thirty species of birds.

One of the most innovative new exhibits to open at the zoo is the **Chimps of Harambee.** The nearly four-acre facility has eight public over-looks, where you can view chimps in forest, meadow, and rock-outcropping settings, all resembling their natural habitat. Indoor viewing also is available. Another hit is the **Penguinarium,** with its new underwater views of the flightless birds. The newest major exhibit is an $8.2-million wildlife interpretive gallery that includes an aquarium of Pacific fish offering a diver's-eye view by minicams, a butterfly and hummingbird garden, and a theater. The zoo's also a great place for a family picnic in its large wooded grove. Adult roller chairs and "kid kabs" are available for rent year-round at the entrance near the gift shop.

The zoo is located at West Ten Mile Road and Woodward Avenue. From Interstate 75 take Interstate 696 west and watch for the zoo directional signs near the Woodward Avenue exit. The park is open year-round and hours vary by season. Admission is $7.50 for ages eighteen to sixty-one, $5.50 for seniors, and $4.50 for children ages two to twelve. Parking is $3.00. For recorded information call (810) 398–0900.

Take your family back to the time when railroad passenger service was the only way to travel with a series of **historic train trips** offered by the **Bluewater Chapter of the National Railway Historical Society.**

You don't have to be a member of the society to join the thousands who have traveled with the group since 1983 in their own classic restored passenger cars behind vintage steam and diesel locomotives.

Trips range from a few hours to overnight journeys with stays and meals at charming hotels in some of the prettiest towns Michigan and surrounding areas have to offer. Many of the single-day trips include special events and tours. Departure and destination points in the past have included Allen Park to Fort Wayne, Indiana, Battle Creek to the lakeside vacation town of Petoskey for a relaxing three-day odyssey, and from Birmingham to Kitchener, Ontario.

Riding the rails is one of the most relaxing ways to travel and is a great way to show your family Michigan's beauty. No one has to worry about missing the scenery while driving or navigating. There are no traffic delays, and you'll often pass sights you can't see from a car window. At the same time, the kids will have a chance to taste the unforgettable romance of rail travel.

One trip that's become almost an annual event is the "Northern Arrow," a four-day journey from Ann Arbor north to Petoskey, in West Michigan on Little Traverse Bay, reminiscent of the nineteenth-century "specials" that carried vacationers north. Passengers enjoy a fall-color preview as they journey to northern Michigan to stay either at a local Holiday Inn, the historic Bay View Inn, or the restored Perry Hotel. Side trips include shopping in Petoskey's historic **Gaslight District,** and optional tours are offered daily. Trips such as this vary in price depending on accommodations chosen and the particular excursion. For information on all trips, call (810) 399–7963.

BLOOMFIELD HILLS

Young children may remember for the rest of their lives their first steps into the planetarium at the **Cranbrook Institute of Science.** It's just one of the treats in store at this mini–natural history museum on the grounds of one of the state's largest and most prestigious private schools.

Nearly a quarter of a million persons annually walk through the institute's exhibits on everything from astronomy to anthropology. The planetarium shows just might lead to your child's first realization that there's something out there bigger than the family backyard or even the neighborhood. As the lights slowly meld to darkness in the eighty-two-seat theater, the star guide takes you on a journey around the Milky Way galaxy, so when those summer nights around the campfire come once again, you can pick out constellations like Orion and the Big Dipper and celestial landmarks like the North Star. Shows change several times a year so chances are your next visit will hold something completely different. The planetarium also presents annual special holiday programs, special events that introduce the heavens to children as young as three, and weekend music and laser shows that are especially popular with teens. The museum's "Nature Place" exhibit houses a collection of live reptiles, including a boa constrictor, and turtles and spiders native to Michigan. In addition, new traveling exhibits from the Smithsonian and other museums appear frequently.

In November the museum presents its annual Native American Days festival. You can watch craft demonstrations, learn how Native Americans used to dress, and even listen to a storyteller relate an Indian legend or two. Other annual events include the Maple Syrup Festival each March, when visitors see the sap flowing from sugar maple trees before its taken to the sugar shack and made into maple candy.

The Gem and Mineral Hall houses a huge display of glittering precious and semiprecious stones, while the Physics Hall is filled with hands-on fun that teaches youngsters about light, movement, air resistance, and lasers. At the gift shop kids can pick out samples of minerals as souvenirs, along with science-related books, and there's also a café serving snacks.

Admission to the museum is $5.00 for adults, with children ages three to seventeen and seniors admitted for $4.00. Children under three enter free. Planetarium shows cost $1.00 more, or $2.00 for the weekend laser light shows. Cranbook is at 1221 North Woodward Avenue (Michigan 1), between Lone Pine and Long Lake roads. The museum is open daily and hours vary; call (810) 645–3200 for specifics. For Laser Show information, call (810) 645–3236.

If you're interested in taking in the skies at home after your planetarium visit, stop by **City Camera** at 6448 Greenfield in Detroit for the city's best selection of telescopes, from inexpensive models to ones costing more than a car for serious stargazers. To reach the shop, exit the Southfield Freeway (Michigan 39) at Warren and travel east approximately 2 miles. The store is one block south on Greenfield on the east side of the street. For information call (313) 846-3922.

ROCHESTER

In the early twentieth century, Detroit was a center of the noveau riche, and the families who ran the mammoth, smoke-belching industrial complexes that put the world on wheels retreated to baronial mansions ringing the city to dine, cavort, and live lives dripping in European-style aristocratic opulence. Now your family can see how the other 1 or 2 percent lived in those days, by touring these historic mansions.

The hundred-room Tudor estate built by the Dodge family is **Meadow Brook Hall,** on the campus of Oakland University. An imposing cut-stone entrance leads into this showplace, which contains twenty-four fireplaces, antiques galore, hand-carved paneling, and an ornate ballroom. You can become an auto baron for the day and treat your family to an overnight stay, or, if you're not feeling quite that moneyed, a tour. The mansion is especially beautiful during the annual Christmas Walk, which runs from late November through early December. Guided tours are given at 1:30 P.M. daily, and in July and August the house is open for public viewing on Mondays through Saturdays from 10:30 A.M. to 5:00 P.M. Be sure to stop in Knoll Cottage, the six-room "playhouse" built for the Dodge children. To reach Meadow Brook, take the Walton Road exit off Interstate 75 and follow the signs. Call (810) 370–3140 for more information.

The Ford Motor Company's namesake and founder, Henry Ford, staked out the western suburbs as his fiefdom, and on the grounds of what is now the University of Michigan at Dearborn he built his mansion, **Fair Lane,** where tours of the estate are offered daily. Ford lived only a few miles from his birthplace, and when he was alive his lands covered some 7,000 acres along the Rouge River. A strong believer in "cottage" industry, he supplied much of his own electrical power from a dam on the river, which also flowed by his famed Rouge industrial complex a few miles away.

The estate's gardens have been totally restored and include the Ford Discovery Trail, a forty-five-minute walking tour with stops at a boathouse along the river; at the estate's oldest living object, a three-hundred-year-old burr oak; and at waterfalls and meadows designed by renowned landscape designer Jens

Jensen. Tours leave at 10:00 and 11:00 A.M. and at 1:00, 2:00, and 3:00 P.M. Monday through Saturday, and every thirty minutes from 1:00 to 4:30 P.M. on Sunday. Admission costs $6.00 for seniors and children between five and twelve; teens and adults pay $7.00. To reach Fair Lane, exit the Southfield Freeway (Michigan 39) at Ford Road and go west to Evergreen; then take Evergreen south and follow the signs. For more details call (313) 593–5590.

On the region's east side, Henry's son, Edsel, and his wife, Eleanor, built their dream house, the sixty-room stone home along Lake St. Clair modeled after stone homes in the Cotswold Hills region of England. Now used for public functions, the **Edsel and Eleanor Ford House** also is open for tours. Of special interest are the eclectic rooms, including a striking art deco den. Tours begin with a fifteen-minute video. To reach the home, leave Interstate 94 at the Vernier/Eight Mile Road exit and turn east. Turn north on Lake Shore Road and head into Grosse Pointe Shores. Tours are offered hourly from noon to 4:00 P.M. on Wednesday through Sunday from April through December, and from 1:00 to 4:00 P.M. the remainder of the year. Admission is $2.00 for children thirteen and under, $3.00 for seniors, and $4.00 for others; call (313) 884–4222.

LAKE ORION

Donuts and baseball? They go together like a ball and glove at **Mickey Lolich's Donut Shop.** When the hero of the Detroit Tigers' win at the 1968 World Series retired in 1977, he went from pitching fastballs to rolling dough balls in Rochester, then built his current shop here in Lake Orion in 1983.

What's unique about it is that it's also a minimuseum devoted to our national pastime, with memorabilia from baseball greats such as Al Kaline and Jim Palmer on display. Lolich, who won three of the seven games played in the '68 Series, also has his bats, baseball cards, and other material on display.

Lolich himself usually can be found in the kitchen, preparing donuts, but he also comes to the counter to visit with customers and sign autographs. To reach his shop, leave Interstate 75 at exit 81 and go north on Michigan 24 to Lake Orion. His place is at 575 North Lapeer Road (Michigan 24), next to the Lake Orion post office. Hours are 5:00 A.M. to 6:00 P.M. Monday through Saturday and 6:00 A.M. to 1:00 P.M. Sunday. For more information, call (810) 693–0029.

WIXOM

Regardless or their age or gender, lots of kids love things mechanical, and in metropolitan Detroit you're in one of the prime places to introduce them to the world of manufacturing by touring an auto plant.

Kids ages twelve and over can watch as steel, glass, and rubber become Lincoln Town Cars, Continentals, and Mark VIIIs at the only factory in the country producing them. The cars are put together in this far western Detroit suburb at the **Ford Motor Company Wixom Assembly Plant.**

Usually lasting two hours, tours start with a fourteen-minute video previewing the steps it takes to build a car. Guides who are retired plant employees then escort groups from the point where unpainted bare metal already stamped in the shape of fenders, doors, or roofs is clamped together and welded to begin the assembly process.

Watch as the parts snake along some of the more than 15 miles of conveyors in the plant to be painted, oven dried, and sent to the final assembly line, where other workers marry them to waiting chassis that have themselves been moving on a conveyor through other parts of the 4.2-million-square-foot plant.

Completed cars then roll off the assembly line at the rate of nearly one a minute to receive final inspection. Plant tours offer a perspective that brings the story of Detroit and the auto down to earth. Tours take place Fridays only and as a result are in constant demand. If you plan to visit the area, write to reserve one of the forty-five spots at least six months in advance or, plant officials say, you'll probably miss your chance. Tours are free. To reserve your space, write Plant Tours, Ford Motor Company Wixom Assembly Plant, 28801 Wixom Road, Wixom, MI 48393–0001. The plant is just off Interstate 94, north of the Wixom Road exit. Call (810) 344–5358 for more information.

MILFORD

Southeastern Michigan's voters were indeed prescient when in 1942 they voted to create and fund a series of parks ringing the city that have become a four-season haven for millions. Today there are more than a dozen parks still-growing in the **Huron-Clinton Metropark system**, which is headquartered near here.

One such in the far western Detroit suburbs is **Kensington Metropark.** Located on an artificial lake backed up by a dam on the Huron River, it's a year-round family attraction that by itself draws millions of users annually. Where else can you sled and toboggan or take cross-country ski lessons in winter, swim and sunbathe in summer at two beaches, and launch your own boat or rent one of several types, including sailboats? In the fall you can enjoy Michigan's sweeping autumn color show by exploring secluded nature trails on your own or joining daily naturalist-guided hikes, climbing aboard the sixty-passenger *Island Queen* paddle wheeler. In spring take the children to witness the annual rite of the season as thousands of waterfowl return to the park's outdoor cen-

ANNUAL EVENTS FOR THE FAMILY IN DETROIT NORTHEAST

Plymouth Ice Sculpture Spectacular, mid-January, Plymouth, (313) 453–1540

Michigan Renaissance Festival, mid-August through September, Holly, (810) 634–5552

Armada Fair, mid-August, Armadda, (810) 784–5488

Romeo Peach Festival, late August through Labor Day, Romeo, (810) 752–4436

Boat Show U.S.A., mid-September, (800) 47–PARKS

ter. Kids can feed the animals at its petting farm as well.

Another example of the metropark system is **Metropolitan Beach,** to the east along Lake St. Clair. On a typical steamy summer weekend day, you'll see thousands of suntan-lotion-soaked bodies on its large beach. A trackless train shuttles families to and from the parking lot and along the 6,600-foot-long boardwalk. Other activities here include the tot lot, where kids as young as age three can ride their bikes without fear of running over a grown-up. At **Wolcott Mill** in Macomb County north of Detroit, discover how an 1847 gristmill works, and at **Lake Erie Metropark,** south of the city, a swimming pool creates waves up to three feet high. A $2.00 daily or $15.00 annual vehicle entry permit is required to enter each park. For a locator map of the parks and their facilities, including seven eighteen-hole golf courses, call (810) 685–1561.

SOUTH LYON

Remember playing capture the flag as a child? You had to avoid the other team while stealthily taking your opponent's pennant and returning to your base? Well, when it comes to the paintball version, whoever captures the flag is the sneakiest and has the best aim.

Paintball carries the kid game one step further, with guns that shoot tiny capsules of paint that splat against your opponents. If one hits you, you're out until the next round.

Since 1983, **Silver Lake Paintball,** the oldest and largest operation of its type in the state, has been catering to the ever-growing numbers who've taken up the sport. Don't get the wrong impression. This is definitely not a paramilitary training area, just a place to let your inner child come out to play. Located on 300 acres with seven all-terrain fields from woods to fake "villages," the facility will rent or sell you all the equipment needed, including body protection and headgear made specially for the sport and either single-splat guns or semiautomatic paintball shooters operated by compressed air. Each session lasts about three hours and teams or groups run through four to five different situations. The objective is to be sneaky enough to capture your opponent's flag, take it back to your station, and hang it up without getting hit by a paintball.

The first hour of each session consists of orientation and handing out equipment. Then you and your friends take the field and the rest of the fun is up to you. Where else can you, your partner, or your children get even with one another in a good-natured way for—take your pick—(a) being grounded the weekend of the big date; (b) not taking out the trash in time; (c) not helping around the house; or (d) all of the above?

Cost for rental of all equipment is about $40 per person, so ask about the frequent discounts or special offers for players who make offpeak reservations. The minimum age to play without parental permission is eighteen, but kids as young as ten can play when parents are present. There are also monthly children's games—only ten- to sixteen-year-olds are allowed to play—and even special dates for Mom. The average player goes through 200 paintballs a session. According to co-owner Kathy Williams, a paintball hit feels a bit like a wet-towel snap, so it's best to wear layered, loose clothing and a neck bandanna.

Games take place rain or shine from early April through early November. An indoor course will provide fun for the rest of the year. Silver Lake Paintball is at 9185 Silverside Road. Exit U.S. 23 south at Silver Lake Road (exit 55) and head east for a mile and a half. After the mobile-home park, veer right as the road splits and go around the lake to the sign. Proceed left ¾ mile on a dirt road to the headquarters. The course is open weekends; call (810) 469–9111 first to reserve your place and obtain more information.

BRIGHTON

Metropolitan Detroit is blessed with plenty of things to do when winter arrives, including skiing at four downhill slopes. While they aren't nearly as high as those in the Rockies or even the state's larger northern resorts, they're among the state's most popular because families can reach them in only a few minutes after getting home from school or work. Ski areas like **Mount Brighton** are also popular because they make it a point to cater to families, whether they're just starting on the bunny hill or are tackling the toughest black-diamond runs.

Those who've never skied before can sign up each winter for the state's annual "Learn to Ski" days. Whether you're seven or seventy-five, the series can break you out of your house in winter to join your family in an activity that's not only fun but will keep you fit as well. The annual program takes youngsters onto the slopes at Brighton and nearly two dozen other areas around the state for beginner lessons.

Since the program is geared to first-time and neophyte skiers, the package also represents a great value. On weekdays from January to mid-February, never-ever skiers can quickly advance their skills, progressing through beginner level lessons taught by a professional instructor. Cost includes all rental equipment and beginner-lift tickets. The package price is far less than the cost of a lift ticket alone, and renting your equipment the first few visits allows you to try out the sport with hardly any investment.

Mount Brighton is one of the most popular teaching resorts in the state. A large and well-trained ski school staff will have your family up and shuffling around on slats within minutes. There are plenty of novice and gentle intermediate runs where you can hone new skills. First you'll learn to walk around on skis, glide a few feet down a very gentle pitch onto a flat area, and do a gliding wedge—the basic "snowplow" stance—down the beginner slope, as well as how to use the chairlifts and tows. Then you'll learn to use the wedge to come to a stop and, ideally, how to turn left or right. Oh, yes, you'll also learn how to get up after you've fallen. (Notice that experienced skiers don't say "if you fall," because you probably will. Everyone does, even the experts.) After the first lesson, you'll be conquering the beginner hill and gaining confidence with every run down.

Skiers should dress properly for the weather. Jeans alone are notorious for wicking up moisture, and a nylon shell over them will prevent snow from melting and then freezing on the fabric. Wear pants that won't wrinkle against your shinbone when tucked into a ski boot; it's a painful experience you won't repeat. And layering is best, starting with synthetic or silk long underwear and a warm jacket over a sweater and shirt or a turtleneck. Avoid long scarves; they can become tangled. And even though many kids will think they won't look cool, put the family in hats. Most body heat is lost through the head. Good gloves—or mittens, which are warmer—are also a must. Contact Mount Brighton for more information on its program by calling (810) 229–9581. Nearly two dozen other Michigan resorts, including Alpine Valley, near Milford, Mount Holly, near Holly, and most others in the southeastern part of the state, also participate in the program. To learn more call the Michigan Travel Bureau at (800) 5432–YES.

CLARKSTON

The granddaddies of all of Michigan's outdoor summer pop music festivals are the **Pine Knob Music Theater** and the neighboring **Meadow Brook Music Theater,** only a few miles away from each other. Pine Knob has been presenting musical entertainment—from the favorite of Parrotheads, Jimmy Buffet, to Sesame Street performers and other children's acts—since the early 1970s. Meanwhile, Meadow Brook has taken a bit higher road, featuring summer performances by the Detroit Symphony, but also bringing in pop and folk artists.

Pine Knob's covered pavilion seats more than 6,400 and the "cheap seats" on the lawn hold more than 8,000. For many concerts, especially the loudest ones, families prefer the lawn seating. Get there early to stake out a spot, spread out a blanket, and chow down on dinner. Often, it seems that folks on the hill don't even care much what group is on stage. They just come for the camaraderie. Beach Boys concerts, for instance, seem to draw a crowd that focuses on who can keep the most beach balls aloft and bouncing among the audience. The season usually runs from mid-May through late September, featuring the gamut from eardrum-breaking hard rock for the teens to blues, country and western, New Age, and folk. Picnic baskets are allowed, but drinks must be purchased in the park if you're eating on the hill. Otherwise, head for one of its picnic areas, or enjoy your own picnic and refreshments at a tailgate party in the parking lot before the show. Pine Knob is reached from several exits off Interstate 75 north of Pontiac, the most popular of which is northbound Sashabaw Road.

Meadow Brook's lawn-seating atmosphere is more genteel. Families heading for the 5,300 lawn seats—actually, like Pine Knob, just a grassy place to spread your blanket—may carry in food and beverages, stretch out, and enjoy music by former Motown greats, folk songs from the likes of Peter, Paul, and Mary, and performances by other popular artists. The uncovered pavilion seating holds 2,200. Both Pine Knob and Meadow Brook cater to families, with free lawn admittance for children twelve and under when accompanied by an adult for select concerts. Meadow Brook is in Rochester Hills, reached off Interstate 75 from University Boulevard. Turn east and follow the signs. For information on both venues, call (810) 377–0100.

HOLLY

Here's your family's chance to dress up without having to wait until Halloween or a costume party. Lords, ladies, squires, and kitchen knaves of all ages flock to the annual **Michigan Renaissance Festival,** held in a wooded glen near the small town of Holly, north of Detroit.

Step back in time at the annual Michigan Renaissance Festival. (Courtesy Michigan Renaissance Festival)

For seven weekends each year beginning in mid-August, the woods come alive with strolling minstrels, knights in shining armor, lords and ladies dressed to the hilt, and plenty of roasted turkey legs, soup in hollowed bread loaves, and other finger food to gnaw on Henry VIII style (remember, this is the sixteenth century: no utensils).

You don't have to come in costume, but it helps everyone get into the mood, especially if you come dressed as a noble family and make the "serfs" bow and scrape as you go by.

More than 150 craftspersons sell their wares, including beautiful walking sticks with sorcererlike faces and other fantasy toppings that are made on the spot. Promenade to the competition ring and watch as knights in more than ninety pounds of armor climb onto horses and stage a mock jousting tourney or engage each other in a one-on-one contest on foot, as the festival's king and queen look on from their royal booths and courtiers nod approvingly at Upson Downs.

A portion of the park is set aside just for children, including human-powered rides to provide not only a laugh but a slight historical insight into what city fairs of yesteryear must have been like. There are daily show performances, games, crafts, puppet shows, and more, including daily sightings of a friendly dragon. Entertainment on the festival's eight theme stages includes jugglers, storytellers, sword swallower, and 200 other costumed performers. Tickets are $12.00 at the gate and about $11.00 in advance for teens and adults. You pay $6.00 ($5.00 in advance) for children five through twelve, and kids under five enter free. The fair is open rain or shine. To reach the grounds, turn off Interstate 75 north at exit 106 near Grand Blanc. Go 2 blocks and turn south onto Dixie Highway for 2 miles. Phone (800) 601–4848 for more information.

WATERFORD TOWNSHIP

It's like hopping on a giant ice cube at **The Fridge,** Michigan's only refrigerated toboggan run, at **Waterford Oaks County Park** north of Pontiac. A unique refrigeration system ices two flumes of water that drop riders 55 feet before they travel another 1,000 feet, flying over hills, straights, and declines. You don't need anything except warm clothes and a readiness to have a blast. Each of the park's 200 toboggans holds four riders (riders must be at least 43 inches tall; those under age eleven must be accompanied by an adult) and are transported by park staff from the finish back to the start. There's a warming building with a fireplace, a viewing area, concessions, and restrooms. Cost is $6.00 for county residents and $8.00 for nonresidents. Hours are 4:00 to 10:00 P.M. weekdays, 10:00 A.M. to 10:00 P.M. Saturday, and 10:00 A.M. to 8:00 P.M. Sunday, weather permitting. The runs are open New Year's Eve and Day but

A toboggan ride down more than 1,000 feet of ice is quite a thrill.

are closed Christmas Eve and Day. The park is located on Scott Lake Road, between Dixie Highway and Watkins Lake Road, near Waterford. To get to the park, leave Interstate 75 at Dixie Highway and head south to Watkins Lake Road. Turn south and follow it to the park. In summers, the park entertains with a wave pool, a BMX bicycling course, and tennis courts. For more information call (810) 858–0906.

SHELBY TOWNSHIP

In the off-season you might just catch a glimpse of Detroit Pistons great Joe Dumars at—where else?—**Joe Dumars' Fieldhouse,** a new concept in a combination play-and-exercise center for both adults and children in this northern Detroit suburb.

If you're in shape, you could participate in ten sports in a row at this 70,000-square-foot complex. In addition to six full-size hardwood-floor indoor basketball courts, there are three outdoors as well, where Dumars hosts regular clinics for children as young as first-graders. The fieldhouse also houses two hardwood volleyball courts and even one where you can play other family members in beach sand regardless of the weather outside. Outdoor beach volleyball courts are open in summer.

Stop having your kids dodge cars in the front yard while they play roller hockey. The fieldhouse has a full-size rink, complete with leagues for kids from eight and under to dads and moms thirty-five and over. After the game head for a workout in the training center.

Once you've had enough, offer the kids a meal at Eat at Joe's, the restaurant serving reasonably priced family fare such as chicken sandwiches, submarines, burgers, and pizza, or head for the sports-themed restaurant/bar and pick up a souvenir at the pro shop on the way. Prices are reasonable. You can rent an indoor volleyball hard court for $6.00 for two hours, or a beach volleyball court for $8.

Joe Dumars' Fieldhouse is at 45300 Mound Road, just north of Michigan 59. To reach it exit Interstate 75 at Michigan 59 and turn east to Mound Road; phone (810) 731-3080.

CHESTERFIELD

Nearby, there's a model railroader's heaven just up the street, where you can see up to ten trains running on 1,000-plus feet of track at the **Lionel Trains Visitor Center,** dedicated to the toy invented by Joshua Lionel in 1901 that still lights the imagination of nearly every American child at Christmastime.

Opened in 1992, the center spotlights the toy trains that have been made here by the Lionel firm since 1986. Like many youngsters, Michigan developer Richard Kughn became enamored of electric trains as a child and of the Lionel brand in particular, and after a disastrous try in Mexico, he bought the company and moved it here.

Free one-hour tours by reservation are offered Tuesday through Sunday. A historical video recounts the company's founding in New York by its namesake and also takes visitors through each step in the process of making the trains. Then, kids, wearing their new free engineer's caps, can join other model train buffs to gawk at the 14-by-40-foot layout with more than 1,000 feet of track supported by 5,000 railroad ties cut and painted by hand. Up to eight trains move simultaneously, switching scale-model rail cars, crossing bridges, and traveling through tunnels and past villages. Visitors can control the action with buttons, working water towers, rail car loaders, and other parts of the intricate layout.

A large display case holds early Lionel memorabilia, and there's a gift shop that sells, among other items, limited-edition boxcars available only at the center, as well as older antique models and rolling stock produced in Michigan now. Lionel is at 26750 23 Mile Road. To reach it take Interstate 94 to exit 243 at New Baltimore and then head left 1 mile to the second light. It's on Russell Smith Drive. Tour times are 10:00 A.M. Tuesday; 10:00 A.M. and 3:00 and 4:00 P.M. Wednesday; 1:30 and 2:30 P.M. Thursday; and hourly from 9:00 A.M. to noon Friday and Saturday. Call (810) 949–4100, extension 1211, to plan a visit.

UTICA

Combine one of the state's largest collection of water slides, a sandy beach on a fifty-six-acre artificial lake, and other waterborne fun and you've got one of Michigan's most popular summer family attractions, **Four Bears Waterpark.** Thousands of families converge here every year to escape the heat and frolic at this watery amusement park less than an hour from downtown Detroit.

Four Bears entertains with miniature golf and a triple-chute water slide that sends kids on a 50-foot-long ride, ending in a splashy landing. Try your hand at the paddle or bumper boats too. Special slides for nonswimming youngsters also help parents teach kids to lose their fear of water.

Out-of-the-water fun for a slight surcharge over regular admission includes go-carts for kids, a golf driving range, and batting cages, where potential sluggers can swing away at softballs or hardballs electrically pitched at varying speeds up to major-league velocity.

Go for an elephant or camel ride before you head for the petting zoo to see the zebras, llamas, chimps, and toucans. There's even a sea lion performance and a bird show. Then, come lunch- or dinnertime, grill out at the four-acre picnic grounds. Don't want to cook? Stop at the Honey Bear restaurant for burgers or chicken.

Four Bears is on Auburn Road between Ryan and Dequindre. Take Interstate 75 to Rochester Road, head north on Rochester for 5 miles, and then turn right on Auburn Road. Go 2½ miles and you'll find the park on the right side. There are no refunds if the lines are long and no rainchecks. Four Bears is alcohol-free and is open from Memorial Day through Labor Day. Admission is $11.95 for those over 48 inches tall, $5.95 for those under 48 inches. Children under age two enter free. In addition, almost daily discounts—such as free admission for moms and grandmothers on Mondays and for fathers and grandfathers on Wednesdays, as well as group rates for families on Friday (five get in for $25)— make Four Bears an even better bargain. Hours are 10:00 A.M. to 3:00 P.M. before June 15 and 11:00 A.M. to 7:00 P.M. thereafter; call (810) 739–5860.

MOUNT CLEMENS

What child isn't ready anytime to tour a candy factory? **Morley Candy Makers** is one of Michigan's largest candy emporiums, because of its popularity among charity fund-raising groups. Morley's cooks its chocolate goodies gallons at a time in huge, old-fashioned copper kettles, just like founder Ervin Morley did in 1919, when he created confections out of his original store in Detroit.

Guided tours are mostly taken by groups, but families can join in if there's room or follow behind and eavesdrop as the guide explains how the plant creates 176 different chocolate-centers in the course of pumping out more than seven tons of goodies each day.

Morley's is especially famed for its sumptuous ice-cream toppings like fudge or chocolate, its boxed candies, and its specialty chocolates like truffles and pecan torties. On hour-long tours of the facility, visitors walk along a 175-foot observation hallway and bask in the aromas of sugar and cocoa as employees and machines dip and mold each of the chocolates, which will eventually be boxed and ready for sale. They learn that caramel is actually the controlled burning of milk, sugar, and cream and that those swirly marks on top of each chocolate identify what kind of center it has. A video also shows what raw cocoa beans and other ingredients look like.

Before you leave the Morley factory, visit the store out front to buy what they've been making. Tours in summer, which start the first Monday after July 4 and continue through Labor Day, are at 10:00 A.M. and 1:00 P.M. Tuesday through Thursday. From then until May 1, they're at 10:00 A.M. and 1:00 and 3:00 P.M. except the week before Easter. The factory and shop are at 23770 Hall Road (Michigan 59). Exit Interstate 94 at the Selfridge Air National Guard Field exit, or Hall Road. Turn west to Gratiot, the first light. Cross Gratiot and look for the signs at the Bavarian Tudor–style building. Call (810) 468–4300 before you visit to see if your family can join another group for a guided tour. If not, your visit will be self-guided and won't include the video.

ARMADA

Every August this small town at the base of Michigan's Thumb welcomes upward of 50,000 visitors to what's generally regarded as Michigan's best county fair. The **Armada Fair** has been crowding 'em in for about 125 years now, and depending on who's bragging, it's either the third- or fourth-oldest county fair in the state. The fun includes everything county fairs should include, from judging the best 4-H sheep, steers, and other four-footed farm inhabitants to the big midway with enough flashing lights to make any child's eyes open wide. But there's more that this fair also brings to the table. Up-and-coming country-and-western stars and other top-name acts entertain in the grandstands each evening, and there are always tractor pulls and other contests. Armada is off Michigan 53, northeast of Romeo in Macomb County. For information on the next edition, call (810) 784–5488.

PORT HURON

A city that's one of Michigan's three portals to Canada, its near southern neighbor—that's right, by a quirk of geography, part of Ontario actually is south of metropolitan Detroit—Port Huron is one of the state's oldest cities, founded in 1686. Originally a fort to protect the entrance to the lower Great Lakes and the French fur trade, it sits where all Great Lakes water funnels into the narrows at the start of the St. Clair River under the Blue Water Bridge.

Port Huron counts Thomas Edison—inventor of the electric light, the movie projector, and the phonograph—among its native sons. Edison once sold newspapers on the train between the city and Detroit. To clue your kids in on local history, stop at the **Port Huron Museum of Arts and History** (810–982–0891), where a small collection of Edison memorabilia is on display. It includes artifacts unearthed from the site of the house where he lived as a boy and performed his first experiments, such as bottles believed to be used by young Edison to store chemicals. Equipment the inventor used in later life at his lab in Menlo Park, New Jersey, including a microscope and bamboo used to make an experimental bulb filament, also are shown. The museum is at 1115 Sixth Street, on the south edge of downtown, one block west of Interstate 69. Admission is $1.50 for adults, $1.00 for seniors, and 50 cents for students. Kids six and under get in free. Museum hours are 1:00 to 4:30 P.M. Wednesday through Sunday.

The same address is the retirement home of the lightship *Huron,* moored along the St. Clair River north of downtown in Pine Grove Park. Until 1970 the *Huron,* actually a floating lighthouse, stood guard to direct ships past shoals north of the St. Clair's treacherous below-bridge currents. Kids can explore the ship to see how its crew of eleven lived aboard the vessel for twenty-one days at a time and learn where else the *Huron* served in its half-century on the lakes. The lightship is open weekends in May, June, and September and Wednesday through Sunday in July and August. Admission is $1.50 for adults, $1.00 for seniors, and 50 cents for students. Children six and under are free. While you're there, the family can also scramble aboard the coast guard cutter *Bramble* for tours.

If you're a sailing family, plan to be here in mid-July to participate in the annual **Blue Water Festival,** which culminates in every sailor's dream race, the annual **Port Huron–Mackinac Island Sailboat Race.** The evening before the starting cannon is fired, the **Black River Harbor** becomes one big floating party as visitors board and mingle with the crew. Other city events include one of the zaniest regattas on the Great Lakes. The mid-August **Cardboard Regatta** takes place on the Black River and all boats must be made of the flimsy material. All manner of craft, from elaborate designs resembling pirate ships to dinghies that don't make it past the dock, try to float down the Black. Before its fateful journey, each entry is displayed downtown.

Where these days can a child watch as workers throw up a huge span linking two countries? Right here in Port Huron. The second **Blue Water Bridge** span is expected to open for traffic in 1997 and it will take more than 14 million pounds of steel to construct it. Sidewalk superintendents can monitor the hard hats' progress from a spot near the present bridge, which, after its twin's completion, will be closed for renovation.

For more on Port Huron's family events, call (800) 852–4242. Port Huron is located at the eastern terminus of Interstate 94.

East Michigan—South

L̶ast Michigan, stretching from the Ohio border to the Straits of Mackinac, is the state's breadbasket. Within its borders farmers tend crops on some of the richest land on earth—giant expanses where flat fields that once grew a portion of the world's largest deciduous forest now grow more dry navy and other beans than any other spot. To the north are some of the state's richest natural resources, from trout-laden streams and reborn forests to the largest limestone quarry in the world. For exploration purposes the region can be divided into north and south, using Michigan 46, which runs east and west, as a divider.

IRISH HILLS

So named by Irish immigrants for the resemblance to their homeland, the **Irish Hills,** located in Michigan's south-central Lower Peninsula, have, since the 1930s, been a one-stop vacation attraction for families. Everything from outdoor fun to quirky, touristy attractions can be found within a few miles of one another along U.S. 12, approximately between Michigan 52 on the east and Coldwater on the west.

Always one of the most popular attractions for families making the short drive from central Michigan and metropolitan Detroit is **Stagecoach Stop USA,** where more than 100,000 visit annually. This re-created frontier town is themed to resemble a Michigan city of the early 1800s, with more than 10,000 antiques gathered by the Bahlau family, from leaded-glass fixtures and a dome that once was the entrance to a downtown Chicago haberdashery to fifty antique carriages, period furniture, and an antique gasoline engine display.

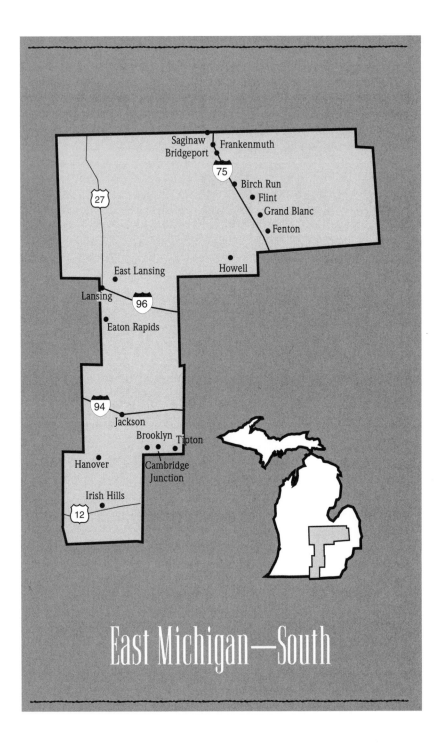

East Michigan—South

Three times a day, the century-old Pawson sawmill, relocated from nearby Devils Lake, fires up to show how wood was cut. Other features include a chapel from the Kentucky hill country.

Stop by the general store for bulk items from candies to peanuts while the kids linger at the petting zoo. Several times in the summer, country-and-western concerts are presented in the 2,000-seat outdoor amphitheater. Stagecoach Stop USA is at 7203 U.S. 12, near Hayes State Park. Admission is $8.00; a $2.00 discount applies to children four to eleven, and tykes three and under are let in for free. The attraction is open weekends in May, and Tuesday through Sunday from June through Labor Day. The saloon, restaurant, and general store are also open Monday. For information call (517) 467–2300.

CAMBRIDGE JUNCTION

For up to seven weekends each summer, the roar of finely tuned stock and Indy car engines that produce more than 900 horsepower each echoes through the heart of Michigan's Irish Hills region at **Michigan International Speedway,** a 2-mile, D-shaped track that rivals anything the South has to offer.

Upwards of 350,000 fans in person and millions more watching television see each of these spectacles of speed. One of the biggest draws is the Marlboro 500, the Motor State's version of the Indy 500 that's billed as the fastest 500-mile race in history. Stock cars also run the track here twice a year, during twin 400-mile races in June and August. Tickets range in price from $20 per person for infield, look-over-someone's-shoulder viewing to between $45 and $65 for seats in the main grandstands on the front straightaway. There's also a special wheelchair platform, as well as a chance for fans who are eighteen and older to walk the pits for $35 (shirt and shoes must be worn and shoulders and legs must be covered.) Area accommodations include a field across from the speedway; camping is free but strictly primitive here, with only central cold water and portable restrooms, so you must be pretty self-sufficient. You can also purchase a pass to the limited, primitive camping area in the infield for $20 per vehicle and an additional $20 per person per day. The track is at 12626 U.S. 12. For more information call (517) 592–6672 or (800) 354–1010.

You can get an inkling of what nineteenth-century stagecoach travel must have been like on the six- to eight-day run along the old Chicago Road (now known as U.S. 12 between Detroit and Chicago) at the **Walker Tavern State Historic Complex,** a restored former overnight inn at the corner of U.S. 12 and Michigan 50.

For years the original inn was known for its famed "Murder Room," the purported scene of what one owner described as a particularly gruesome crime involving a stolen money belt. The cash was later reported to have been buried on the grounds and was the object of scores of secretive nighttime searches by locals—netting nothing but holes in the yard. According to the same owner, the inn hosted such famous guests as frontier author James Fenimore Cooper and Daniel Webster. State officials later surmised that these tales were hoaxes perpetrated by the inn's proprietor, who thought they'd be good for business. (He was right, of course.)

Annual events include a Civil War encampment and, in mid-August, "Industry Days" showing how settlers lived and produced their own goods on what then was the western frontier. A movie at the visitors center on travel in the 1840s depicts a young boy's journey from New York to Chicago, including an overland ride on a much more rugged U.S. 12 than today's paved version. At the tavern you'll enter the mudroom, where guests dusted themselves off from the stage ride and signed in for the night. In the parlor, the women gathered to relax at night, while the men repaired to the bar, where females weren't allowed. The tavern, which held 150 persons, also served as a post office and, on Sunday mornings, a church.

Walker Tavern is open Memorial Day through Labor Day, from 11:30 A.M. to 6:00 P.M. Wednesday through Sunday. For information on the historic complex, call (517) 467–4414. Actually, you can see two taverns. The **Walker Brick Tavern,** built to replace the original, is an antiques market located across the street—one of scores you'll find along U.S. 12 here.

A few miles down the road, at the **Prehistoric Forest, Jungle Rapids Water Slide and Mystery Hill,** you can see depictions of more than fifty life-size dinosaurs on a forty-minute miniature-train ride, including some that move and bellow. Kids can run through a maze and find the three dinosaurs leading to the way out, then jump onto the 400-foot-long water slide. At Mystery Hill, tour guides take you to a spot where you'll see water running uphill and other illusory feats. These attractions are located at 8108 U.S. 12, a quarter-mile west of Hayes State Park. Admission price varies by activity. For specifics call (517) 467–2514. Other fun kid things to do in the Hills include prerequisite go-cart and bumper boat attractions, and climbing the old twin **Irish Hills Observation Towers** to admire the scenic views a mile west of U.S. 12 and Michigan 124; call (517) 467–2606 for information.

HANOVER

Here's a chance to show your kids a bit of living American history. In the late 1800s the American bison, or buffalo, was on the edge of extinction, reduced in an ongoing slaughter from the thirty to fifty million that once roamed the continent, in nearly every region, to fewer than 1,000. The future of the buffalo is now secure, however, thanks mostly to private herd ranchers like Gary Childs, owner of the **Childs' Place Buffalo Ranch** in the heart of Michigan's Irish Hills.

A native Michigander with his heart in the West, Childs was always intrigued by the woolly, 2,000-pound beasts. Instead of moving to Wyoming or Montana to watch the buffalo roam, he started his own local herd and now takes care of up to fifty "buffs." Visitors can climb aboard a hay wagon hitched to a tractor and ride into his pastures to help feed the huge animals ears of corn, and kids can actually reach out from the wagon to touch them.

Childs also sells buffalo meat, which he calls nature's original health food. Buffalo is lower in fat, cholesterol, and calories and higher in protein than beef. Moreover, these bison are raised free of chemicals and added hormones. In addition to the animal's meat, Childs uses just about everything else but the grunt, much as Native Americans once did on the plains. Bones are sold for jewelry, hides for coats, moccasins, and rugs. Native Americans often visit to purchase ceremonial items.

Like the Native Americans who sang songs of praise to the buffalo, Childs pays homage to his bread and butter with an annual **Buffalo Rendezvous** in mid-May. Visitors encounter "living history" portrayals of Abraham Lincoln, Buffalo Bill, and General George A. Custer. Native Americans perform dances and tell legends, cowboys camp in the backyard, and Childs serves up buffalo burgers. Come mid-July Childs also hosts a real, old-fashioned, one-day **Rodeo** that draws more than two hundred competitors and upwards of 2,000 fans. A visit to his herd and the Rendezvous costs $4.00 per person. The rodeo is $8.00 for adults and teens, $4.00 for children six through twelve, and free for younger kids. The Childs ranch is at 12770 Roundtree Road. Take U.S. 12 to Moscow Road, go north to Mosherville Road, and turn west to Roundtree; then go north and follow the signs. Call (517) 563–8249 for more information.

TIPTON

It's said that Michigan State University's East Lansing campus is one of the nation's most beautiful because of its greenery, and the university continues that tradition in **Hidden Lake Gardens,** just east of the other Irish Hills attractions. Inside this 755-acre complex, a 6-mile one-way drive takes you through a lush arboretum featuring thousands of trees, nearly all of them labeled, 100-plus acres of plants and shrubs, and displays of special dwarf evergreens. Under a tropical greenhouse dome, walk past plants from across the world. Show your kids what coffee plants and cocoa evergreens look like, or other trees from the tropics, like bamboo. Nearby, the "All America" display garden features hundreds of more familiar plants from azaleas to shrubs. The kids can lean out the car window and soak in a lesson in biology while you rest up from the Irish Hills' other attractions. Or, if you've still got some energy, climb out and explore the gardens' 5 miles of nature trails, one of which accommodates wheelchairs. There's also a picnic area. Hidden Lake Gardens is located 2 miles west of Tipton on Michigan 50. Admission is $1.00 per person on weekdays and $3.00 on weekends. Hours are 8:00 A.M. to dusk. For information call (517) 431–2060.

JACKSON

Fountains and other watery displays have always been a part of Michigan's towns, and one of the most spectacular in the state is the **Cascades at Sparks Foundation County Park.** Called the Cascades for short, it's named for former mayor and Jackson industrialist William "Cap" Sparks, who donated the land for the park. The fountain that bears his name is modeled after one he saw in Barcelona, Spain.

The oldest of its type in the Western Hemisphere, the 500-foot-long, 64-foot-high structure has delighted families since 1932 as it gushes water over sixteen falls and three main pools, while lights color the tableau with an unending changing palette, all set to music.

You can watch the display from an amphitheater or follow a footpath to take in the scene from love seats only a few feet from the spray. The show goes on nightly from Memorial Day to Labor Day weekend. It's only one of the highlights of the park, which also contains two golf courses, minigolf, picnic areas, batting cages, paddleboats, and the **Cascades Museum,** where photos trace the history of the building of the fountain.

Special theme weekends include an August Civil War muster billed as the Midwest's largest. Park admission is $5.00 per person; children under five are free. To find the Cascades, turn off Interstate 94 at Cooper Street (exit 183), go south, and follow the signs. For more information call (517) 788–4320.

It's only a 2-mile drive from the Cascades to the **Ella Sharp Museum,** a 530-acre site filled with historic local structures and living history demonstrations around the nineteenth-century home of Ella Sharp, who willed the property to the city. There's a one-room school, woodworking shop, and other buildings that have been moved to the site, including a log house and doctor's office. Special seasonal events are held in March, October, and December, when the Sharp residence is decorated for a Victorian Christmas.

The visitors center connects to a modern-art gallery and to a restaurant located inside the original farm granary that's open for lunch Tuesday through

BILL'S TOP FAMILY ADVENTURES IN EAST MICHIGAN–SOUTH

1. The Cascades at Sparks Foundation Park, Jackson
2. Michigan Space Center, Jackson
3. State Capitol and Michigan Historical Center, Lansing
4. Irish Hills, Route 12
5. The town of Frankenmuth

Saturday. Museum hours are Tuesday to Friday from 10:00 A.M. to 4:00 P.M., and weekends from 11:00 A.M. to 4:00 P.M.; it's closed Monday and holidays. Admission is $2.50 for adults, $2.00 for seniors, and $1.00 for children ages five to fifteen. The museum is at 3225 Fourth Street. Get off Interstate 94 at Cooper Street (exit 183) and head south. Turn west onto Prospect, then south onto Fourth Street. For more information call (517) 787–2320.

After you're through giving the kids a history lesson, it's treat time. Jackson proclaims proudly that the Republican party was founded there. Now what can be more American than that? Ice cream, of course.

According to voters of all political persuasions, one of the state's best places to sink your teeth into a triple-decker chocolate-banana sundae is the **Parlor in the All-Star Dairy,** on the city's northwest side. For fifty years, the summer weekends have found the dairy parking lot choked with cars as lovers of sweet confections share ice cream, whipped cream, fudge, or a score of other toppings on their wish-fulfillment list. An estimated 700 gallons of ice cream is devoured weekly.

The huge menu lists nearly two dozen different sundaes and fountain specials, parfaits, and splits—you name it, they'll make it. The pièce de résistance, if you dare, is twenty-one different flavors topped with everything in the place, for $14.95.

The most popular item is the pecan combo sundae—vanilla ice cream drizzled with caramel fudge and sprinkled with pecans—for $3.45. A "single" cone, actually two scoops, is $1.10, plus tax. The parlor opens at 11:00 A.M. daily, and closes at 11:00 P.M. on Friday and Saturday, as well as on every night from Memorial Day to Labor Day; the rest of the time it shuts down at 10:00

P.M. To reach Jackson, leave Interstate 94 at exit 138 and go south six stoplights. At the sixth, turn west onto Wildwood, go two more lights, and veer to the right onto Daniel. The ice cream shop is at 1401 Daniel Road; call (517) 782–7141.

After filling up on ice cream, give your family a glimpse of the recent past and what the future will hold at the **Michigan Space Center,** on the campus of Jackson Community College.

Why a space center in Michigan, and particularly in Jackson? It was dedicated in 1977 to honor the several astronauts and other Michigan citizens who have played prominent roles in the nation's space program, including those who had connections with the city, such as Al Warden, who was born and raised here, James McDivitt, and Jack Lousma.

Your first taste of what's in store is an 85-foot-tall Mercury Redstone launch vehicle (space talk for rocket), the same kind used to launch Mercury project astronauts—and made in Michigan. Inside the space center's gold-colored dome, exhibits include the *Apollo 9* command module, which was sent into earth orbit in March 1969 under McDivitt's command to test the lunar excursion module that four months later carried astronauts to the moon's surface for the first time. The suit he wore on the mission also is displayed.

Kids can even climb inside a mock Mercury capsule, the type America's first astronauts rode into low earth orbit. There's also a memorial to the ill-fated crew of the shuttle *Challenger.* In the theater you'll see either *Reflections,* a film based on the *Apollo 9* flight, or, if the space shuttle is orbiting earth, live broadcasts direct from the crew's quarters. Hours from Memorial Day to Labor Day are 10:00 A.M. to 5:00 P.M. Tuesday through Saturday and Sunday from noon to 5:00 P.M. Call (517) 787–4425 for hours after Labor Day. Admission is $3.85 for adults, $2.75 for students and seniors. An $11.00 family pass is also available, and children five and under are free. To get to the space center from Interstate 94, take exit 142, head south on U.S. 127 and go 6 miles to the Michigan 50 exit. Turn west onto McDevitt Avenue (a sign painter spelled his name wrong, and it's never been changed) to the first traffic light; then turn south onto Hague Avenue, travel 2 miles to Emmons Road, and follow the signs to the center.

EAST LANSING

The hometown of Michigan State University has the gamut of family fun, from festivals to strolling one of the nation's most beautiful campuses. First, though, you can forget all the other city festivals you've been to or heard about. East Lansing's **Michigan Festival** will no doubt top 'em all.

Actually, there are two festivals in one. Entertainers from Dolly Parton to the Preservation Hall Jazz Band to Gladys Knight have appeared on the main stage during the weeklong event. Downtown, one block of Grand River is filled with truckloads of sand, turning it into a beach for volleyball and other fun, and hundreds of vendors provide the eats. The festival within a festival, the Festival of Michigan Folklife, will introduce your youngsters to crafts and daily activities in the state during the eighteenth century. To learn what's in store for this year—the citywide block party occurs in mid-August—call (800) 648–6630.

And you thought college campuses were only for eighteen-to-twenty-one-year-olds. Think again. If you've got a precollege-age youngster who's ready to pick a school or you just want to go back and relive a bit of your youth, East Lansing's **Michigan State University campus** makes a perfect weekend getaway. It's considered one of the nation's most picturesque and beautiful college venues. Some liken it to going to school in an arboretum, so majestic are the huge oaks, maples, and pines that cover the old part of the campus.

At the north campus end are the **W. J. Beal Botanical Gardens** and at the south end, the new, seven-acre **MSU Horticultural Demonstration Gardens.** Classrooms and older dorm buildings are draped in ivy for that perfect campus look. At the Red Cedar River, which flows between the buildings, join the students taking a study break and rent a canoe for a leisurely float.

Then join the kids in an ice cream or yogurt or take home some cheese from the **MSU Dairy Store** on Farm Lane. Is two scoops of creamy delight for under a buck cheap enough? Near **Beaumont Tower,** which plays carillon concerts, is the **MSU Museum,** with lots of natural history exhibits, including dinosaur fossils and Michigan history; or head for the **Kresge Art Museum** for an education in 5,000 years of art. In the evening take in a concert or play at the **Wharton Center for the Performing Arts,** site of one of the 1992 presidential debates.

You can become even more familiar with what the campus offers by renting a student for a free tour. In downtown East Lansing, stores catering to students along Grand River Avenue sell everything from MSU-logo clothing to books. Several good restaurants are in the area as well. To reach East Lansing take Interstate 96 to Interstate 496 north and follow the signs to the main campus exit, Trowbridge Road. For free information on the entire Lansing/East Lansing region, call (800) 968–8474. To book a student tour, call (517) 355–4458.

LANSING

What do politics and cat litter have in common? Find out by traveling a mile or so west to downtown Lansing, the state capital. You can start here by taking your kids on a tour of Michigan's recently renovated **State Capitol.**

Tour guides tell more than 100,000 visitors each year of the work to save the once-crumbling 1879 building in time for the state's 150th birthday. Tours show how the original builders used Michigan's vast forests to save taxpayers money. White pine was painted to resemble marble and walnut. In the House and Senate galleries, look up at the seals of each state. To obtain the proper luster, guides will tell you, restorers rubbed much of the woodwork with a mix of cat litter and beer, somehow appropriate for these chambers. In the rotunda you can view portraits of former state governors. The free, thirty-minute tours are offered from 9:00 A.M. to 4:00 P.M. Monday through Friday and from noon to 4:00 P.M. on weekends. To reach the Capitol take Grand River Avenue west from the MSU campus. Call (517) 373–2353 for information.

Only a block west of the Capitol, the **Michigan Library and Historical Center** is the place to be if you want to introduce your family to state history. A three-story topographical map of the state climbs one lobby wall of the Historical Center. Inside, trace the state's history, from Native Americans onward. There's even a replica of an Upper Peninsula copper mine. A new permanent exhibit, "Michigan in the Twentieth Century," opened in 1995, featuring everything from a Ford Model T, a 1950s-era bathroom, and a re-created portion of the 1957 Detroit Auto Show.

Next door, visit the Library, which houses one of the top ten genealogical archives in the nation. There are more than 300,000 donated photos, personal papers, and diaries. The complex is at 717 West Allegan Street, three blocks southwest of the Capitol. It is open from 9:00 A.M. to 4:30 P.M. Monday through Friday, from 10:00 A.M. to 4:00 P.M. Saturday, and from 1:00 to 5:00 P.M. Sunday. Admission is free. Call (517) 373–3559 for more information.

Just a few blocks to the east of the Capitol is one of the best collections of museums in any town, not just in Michigan. The **Impression 5 Museum** is the state's largest hands-on children's museum and was judged one of the country's top ten. There's something here for everyone from tots to teens, with demonstrations on computers, natural sciences, medicine, and physics, including a special exhibit on the fish of the Grand River, which flows just outside. Kids can freeze their shadows on a wall, try to grab a hologram, or explore their senses among the 200 exhibits. The museum is at 200 Museum Drive and is open from 10:00 A.M. to 5:00 P.M. Monday through Saturday, and from noon to 5:00 P.M. on Sunday. Admission is $4.50 for adults and $3.00 for seniors and for children ages four to eighteen; call (517) 485–8116. Almost next door, the **R. E. Olds Museum,** at 240 Museum Drive, focuses on the Lansing inventor whose cars eventually joined the stable of the General Motors Corporation

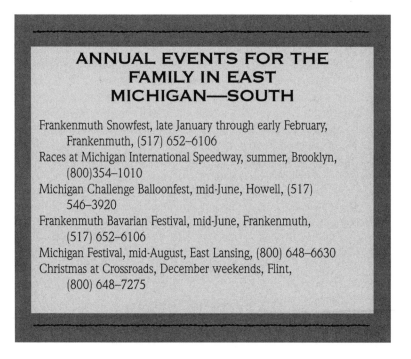

ANNUAL EVENTS FOR THE FAMILY IN EAST MICHIGAN—SOUTH

Frankenmuth Snowfest, late January through early February, Frankenmuth, (517) 652–6106

Races at Michigan International Speedway, summer, Brooklyn, (800)354–1010

Michigan Challenge Balloonfest, mid-June, Howell, (517) 546–3920

Frankenmuth Bavarian Festival, mid-June, Frankenmuth, (517) 652–6106

Michigan Festival, mid-August, East Lansing, (800) 648–6630

Christmas at Crossroads, December weekends, Flint, (800) 648–7275

(they are still produced in the city). Antique and other notable autos, from some of the first Oldsmobiles made to the fastest, are displayed. The smaller **Michigan Museum of Surveying,** at 220 Museum Drive, is unique in the country and is a must for technical types interested in tools of that trade. Admission is free, and it's open from 1:00 to 5:00 P.M. Tuesday through Friday and from noon to 4:00 P.M. on Sunday; call (517) 484–6605. A short drive away on the banks of the Grand River, the **Michigan Women's Historical Center and Hall of Fame** celebrates women's role in building the state. Don't miss its gallery featuring works by prominent Michigan women artists. The center is at 212 West Main and is open Wednesday through Friday from noon to 5:00 P.M. and Sunday from 2:00 to 4:00 P.M. Admission is $1.00 for students, $2.00 for seniors, and $2.50 for others; call (517) 484–1880.

What better way to finish a tour of the capital than with a ball game? Starting in 1996, the state capital will ring with the crack of the bat and howl of the crowd as the city welcomes its own baseball team, curiously named the **Lansing Lugnuts.** A Class A Midwest League farm club for the Kansas City Royals, the Nuts came from Springfield, Illnois. Their new home will be a 6,000-

seat downtown stadium close to the Capitol. Special promotions during the season will include chances to win a car and on-field contests. In addition to the permanent seats, two tiered grassy areas will have room for 4,000 more fans behind right and left fields. For ticket and schedule information, call (800) 945–6887.

An industry tour perhaps unique in the Midwest is available at Michigan's only aircraft factory, located on the grounds of Lansing's **Capital City Airport.** The Waco biplane design has been flying since the 1930s, but after years of its being out of production, company owners thought there'd be a market for an updated version of this fast, highly maneuverable, reliable plane. Were they ever right. Selling at more than $100,000 a copy, there's a considerable waiting list. You'll watch as each plane is hand-built in this small factory, where the fabric-covered fuselage and wings are formed and "doped" the old-fashioned way. Any family member who's ever built model airplanes will be amazed at how similarly the real thing is constructed. After visiting the factory you can go out to the Waco hangar at the airport to see the gleaming, lacquered finished product. Tours are free. The airport is north of downtown off Grand River Avenue. For tour information call (517) 321–7500.

EATON RAPIDS

Even if you're just a Saturday-afternoon, around-the-neighborhood bicycle rider, you owe an adventure to yourself and your family. Sign up just once for this ride, which takes you from the farmlands of central Michigan to the pine forests of the north, culminating in an afternoon ride across the 5-mile-long Mackinac Bridge under pedal power, the only time it's permitted, during the **DALMAC** ride. Standing for Dick Allen Lansing to Mackinac Classic, the 300-mile-plus pedal is the oldest organized long-distance bike ride in the state.

It began in 1970 when then State Senator Dick Allen wanted to bring attention to the growing need for bicycle routes. Originally, the ride started each Labor Day at the Capitol in Lansing. But DALMAC has gotten too big over the years. Now, the four-day trek's 1,600 spots fill by early spring. Take your pick of four routes, including the "four-day quad," four days of 100 miles each, or a five-day trip of 100 miles daily. Bikes camp in schools and parks en route. Don't worry about your camping gear. Trucks carry it all. On the last day, bikers travel across the bridge in packs, and the next morning they can join the 70,000 or so others in the annual Mackinac Bridge Walk.

The ride can be as strenuous or relaxing as you make it, and bikers as young as eight or nine have gone the distance. For information on signing up through DALMAC headquarters, in Eaton Rapids, just south of Lansing, call (517) 339–1758.

HOWELL

The sport of hot-air ballooning takes over the skies of southern Michigan each summer. Besides a number of festivals, you'll find places where you can book a flight or two yourself.

In the small town of Howell, about 20 miles east of Lansing, nearly 60,000 ballooning fans converge for the **Michigan Challenge Balloonfest,** which takes over the area around Howell High School the third weekend of every June. Skydiving demos, stunt kites, art exhibits, music, antique cars, and fireworks are topped off by mass ascensions of nearly sixty giant, colorful balloons each evening, as they compete for the Michigan Challenge Trophy. To reach the high school, take Interstate 96 exit 133 or 137 and follow the signs. Admission is just $7.00 per carload. For more information call the Howell Area Chamber of Commerce at (517) 546–3920.

FENTON

To the east, take your family walking the winds and get a bird's-eye view of the state's scenic landscape, lakes, and wildlife the way the pros do aboard an aerial nature trek with **Captain Phogg of the Balloon Corporation of America.** The most popular package is "the traditional." From a private launch field on Grange Hall Road, up to eight persons can join the pilot on an hour-long flight wherever the winds take you, setting down in another field and ending with a ballooning tradition, a champagne celebration. The traditional flight is $179 per person. Treat your sweet to the sweetheart package, an hour-long, private charter flight, for $250 per person. Captain Phogg flies twice daily, seven days a week, except Christmas Day. To get to Captain Phogg, take Interstate 75 to exit 101, Grange Hall Road. Turn west, go about 4 miles to Holly, and continue through the traffic light. Watch for a flashing yellow light at Fish Lake Road; the entrance is 200 yards past the light on the south. For information call (810) 634–3094.

GRAND BLANC

Time was when the farmlands around the Fenton–Grand Blanc–Flint area teemed with the sounds of cackling rooster pheasants. Entire school systems declared holidays for Michigan's pheasant season opener; but since the 1950s urban sprawl and new farming methods practically wiped out the natural populations. While they're slowly coming back, you can still bag a bird or two at hunting sanctuaries like **Mitchell Farms Pheasant Preserve.** In the early 1990s the Mitchell boys changed their great-grandfather's nearly century-old farm south of Flint into a ten-month opportunity not only for hunting pheasant but for wildlife viewing as well. Sons and fathers, fathers and daughters, wives and husbands each day traipse across eight different fields containing more than 500 acres in cover ranging from corn to willow stands and marshes. The farm each year goes through approximately 14,000 pheasant chicks, which are raised in state-approved pens and then released to roam the hunting fields. The success rate for landing one of these lively birds is much less than you'd imagine, ranging from 10 to 60 percent on average. In the fields you'll not only see pheasants but hawks, owls, fox, deer, and even coyotes, barely 10 miles from a city of 140,000. Memberships per calendar year are $150 and include wives and children under age twenty-one. A small clubhouse serves as a registration and warming room. Trial memberships are $25 per person, which goes toward regular membership. Birds are $18 apiece with a minimum of four birds per party. The club is 4 miles east of the U.S. 23 Thompson Road exit to McWain. Off Interstate 75, take Holly Road, exit 108, south to a stop sign. Turn west on Baldwin Road for 5 miles; then go left on McWain Road. For more information call (810) 694–2281.

FLINT

The whole of this city's history is tied in some way to the wheel. First there were the carriage shops of downtown, which gave birth to the largest automotive company in the world. General Motors remains a huge presence in this town, nicknamed the Vehicle City, despite downsizing, with upwards of 50,000 still working in its plants. On a free tour your kids can get their first glimpse of what it's like to work in an auto plant. Step inside the giant **Buick City** complex, where the Buick LeSabre and Oldsmobile 88 start as jumbles of parts at one end and are driven out at the other. Buick City is at 902 East Hamilton, north of downtown. From Interstate 75, take Interstate 475 north and exit at Davison/Hamilton roads. Turn west onto Davison and at the third light turn south onto Industrial. The headquarters is at the corner of Industrial and Hamilton. To arrange a tour call (810) 236–4494. At the **General Motors Truck and Bus Plant,** watch as GM's Crew Cab pickups roll off the line. Walking tours take about sixty to ninety minutes, and you'll see the process of assembling the family car from start to finish. Children under five are not allowed on the tour and you must wear close-toed shoes. Safety glasses are loaned at the start. The plant is at G-3100 Van Slyke. To reach it exit U.S. 23 at Bristol Road; turn north onto Van Slyke and then west into the parking lot at the third light. For reservations call (810) 236–4978. Call in advance for both plants, as model changeovers and other factors may disrupt tours, and summer-month tours can fill far in advance. Reservations are a must.

Now head for 711 North Saginaw Street to see the other side of the story at the **Labor Museum and Learning Center of Michigan.** The museum is unique, devoting its displays to the story of working men and women, including the birth of the United Auto Workers at the infamous 1936–37 Flint sit-down strike, when employees took over a plant and endured tear gas bombings and hunger to force GM to recognize their rights and bargain for better wages. Radio recordings from the 1930s of those who protested tell the story in their own words. Museum hours are Tuesday to Friday from 10:00 A.M. to 5:00 P.M. Admission is free for children under twelve, $1.00 for seniors and students, and $2.00 for others. The museum is reached by exiting Interstate 475 at Longway Boulevard and heading west for 6 blocks; it's on the south side. For information call (810) 762–0251.

Everything from a steam-train ride through the countryside—complete with a visit by mock robbers every hour—to a look at what everyday life in the Flint area was like back in the 1860s is in store at **Historic Crossroads Village.** The complex is part of the Genesee County parks system. Inside, craftspersons demonstrate blacksmithing, spinning, woodworking, and how mothers managed cooking with the right heat on woodstoves. Twenty-nine historic buildings make up the village. Kids will especially enjoy the 1910-era Ferris wheel and 1912 carousel. The steam-train ride aboard the **Huckleberry Railroad** lasts about thirty-five minutes and is the state's only authentic narrow-gauge line. The park is also the site of the annual **Michigan Storytellers Festival** in mid-July, when the state's best yarn-spinners come to tell of the state's past—some scary tales and some with historical truths. During the holidays, the village is festooned with more than 300,000 festive lights during **Christmas at Crossroads,** weekends from Thanksgiving through December 30. Regular admission for the train ride and village is $8.25 for adults, $5.50 for children ages four through twelve, and $2.25 for seniors. Children under four get in free. Crossroads Village is at G-6140 Bray Road; exit Interstate 475 at exit 13 (Saginaw Street) and follow the signs. Summer hours are 10:00 A.M. to 5:30 P.M. Monday through Friday and 11:00 A.M. to 6:30 P.M. on weekends. Christmas at Crossroads hours are from 3:30 to 9:30 P.M. Call (800) 648–7275 for details.

BIRCH RUN

There are five other factory-discount-outlet malls in Michigan, but for anyone's money, **The Outlets at Birch Run** is by far the largest, offering markdowns on everything from books to toys to tools to brand-name clothes you'll otherwise find only at standard retail malls. True, some items are damaged and some are closeouts, but many are only last season's line or production overruns from this season.

Families, especially around the big summer holiday sidewalk sales, spend the entire day roaming the 175 stores. You can pick up school shoes for the kids at Nike, luggage for your next trip at American Tourister, and book bags at Eddie Bauer, and then shop for clothes at scores of other stores.

If you get hungry, there are shops selling everything from real food to fudge—even one for Pepperidge Farm cookie aficionados. Open since 1986, the mall even provides a trolley between its sections. The mall is open from 10:00 A.M. to 9:00 P.M. Monday through Saturday and 11:00 A.M. to 6:00 P.M. Sunday. Exit Interstate 75 at Birch Run and follow the flying charge cards. For information call (517) 624–9348.

A few miles to the east, one of the newest and best exhibits in the state introduces young children to the animal kingdom. More than sixty different species from around the world can be seen from gravel trails that weave throughout thirty-eight acres of woods at the **Wilderness Trails Animal Park.** Show your youngsters everything from black bears, which roam wild barely an hour's drive north, to coyotes, raccoons, otters, and porcupines. More exotic types you'll see include lions, llamas, and even a Siberian brown bear. There are two walking paths. A half-mile trail takes you past the front part of the exhibits, while a back trail allows you to see many of the hoofed animals, such as elk and deer (you can see those in the wild in northern Michigan, too), that may be too shy to be seen from the other. You pay 50 cents per person and hop aboard the horse-drawn covered wagon that takes twenty visitors per trip on half-hour tours of the entire facility. In addition to a petting area where children can see, feed, and touch baby animals, there's also a small picnic area and playground. Eventually, park organizers will add cross-country ski trails so the facility can be enjoyed fully even in winter. Wilderness Trails is at 11721 Gera Road (Michigan 83), about 2½ miles east and north of the Interstate 75 Birch Run exit. After exiting, turn east, follow the road to the Michigan 83 intersection, and turn north; the park is ¼ mile north, on the east side of the road. Admission is $5.00 for teens and adults, $4.00 for children three through twelve, and for anyone two or under, free. Summer hours are 10:00 A.M. to 6:00 P.M. Monday through Friday and 10:00 A.M. to 8:00 P.M. on weekends. In winter the park is open from 10:00 A.M. to 4:00 P.M. daily except Wednesday, weather permitting. For information, call (517) 624–6177.

BRIDGEPORT

Rain or shine, after or before hitting Birch Run, treat the kids to a ride on the world's largest one-quarter-size railroad, **Junction Valley,** just east of the Saginaw suburb of Bridgeport. Climb aboard the miniature cars as one of eight scale model diesel locomotives pulls you on the 2-mile ride through woods, over 865 feet of trestles, including the only "diamond crossing trestle" in the world, and even through a 100-foot-long tunnel. There's also a picnic area and a play-ground. The season starts the weekend before Memorial Day, and special events take place regularly, including a Christmas program and Halloween spook train rides past thirty-five different scenes, to the light of more than 250 trackside jack-o-lanterns. It's "All aboard!" on the railroad seven days a week through Labor Day weekend, from 10:00 A.M. to 6:00 P.M. Monday through Saturday and from 1:00 to 6:00 P.M. on Sunday. The train operates weekends-only from September through October 8, between 1:00 and 5:00 P.M. Admission is $4.00 for adults and teens, $3.25 for children ages two to twelve, and $3.75 for seniors. The line is at 7065 Dixie Highway at Junction Road. To reach the rails, exit 144 off Interstate 75 and head south on Dixie Highway 2 miles to the first flashing traffic light. For more information call (517) 777–3480.

FRANKENMUTH

Barely five minutes east of the railroad, you can enter the realm of gemütlichkeit, that untranslatable German word that can mean everything from hospitality to down-home friendly. Whatever your interpretation, **Frankenmuth** will supply.

Founded in the early 1800s by Germans who came to this then-wilderness to preach to Native American tribes, the town has held on to its German past while transforming itself into Michigan's top tourist destination.

Whatever the season or the reason, it seems there's almost always a cel-ebration going on, from the weeklong mid-June **Bavarian Festival** that draws more than 100,000 for food, parades, and lots of polka music to the late-January-early-February **Zehnder's Snow Fest,** which brings a like number to view massive snow sculptures thrown up around the town's two famous downtown restaurants, **Zehnder's,** renowned for family-style chicken, and the **Bavarian Inn,** serving German-style meals. Each, incidentally, is owned by Zehnder family members. Snow sculptures also line Main Street, where there

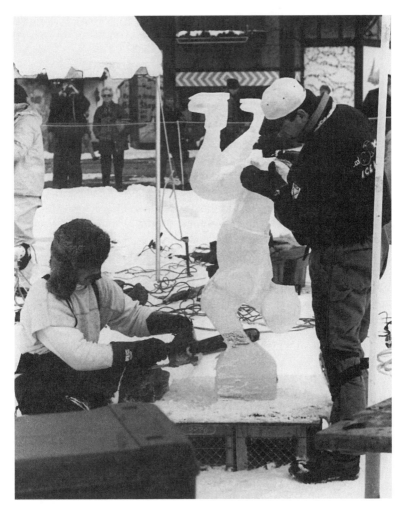

One of the intricate ice sculptures on display during Frankenmuth's Snow Fest.

are nearly fifty shops, selling everything from fresh-ground flour and hand-carved chess sets to made-while-you-shop dolls for the kids.

Just up the street from the restaurants, take a short tour that explains how barley, water, yeast, and hops—the only ingredients used, according to ancient German brewing laws—become beer at the **Frankenmuth Brewing Company,** which has been making suds here since 1862. To reach Frankenmuth, take Junction Road east to Michigan 83. The main business district runs southward from there. For more information on all the town's attractions, call (517) 652–6106.

SAGINAW

When the temperature drops here, it's the signal for hundreds of locals and tourists to come into the cold during the annual **Shiver on the River,** the downtown fishing festival that not only celebrates renewed annual runs of hungry walleyes, but includes a contest to catch the biggest walleye through the ice of the Saginaw River and its main tributaries. Each year the fish swim into the river from Saginaw Bay to winter and then spawn in spring.

There's usually a top prize of nearly $1,000 for the heaviest walleye, and some years there's a special award for any angler who catches a fish that sets a state record. Walleyes up to ten pounds are commonly pulled up through the ice here. If you come for the fun of it or to teach your offspring this unique brand of fishing, all the equipment you'll need is a license, a stubby ice-fishing rod, an auger or spike to chip a hole through the ice, and warm clothes, including gloves or mittens and, especially, boots. If you're in it for the money, get the rules and fill out an entry blank for $5.00 at local tackle shops, and head out. Best fishing times are usually early morning and late evening. Weigh-ins are all conducted at the Huron Fish Company, 505 Gratiot, in Saginaw. For more information call (517) 776–9704.

If you've never taken your kids on a real adventure, there's one waiting just down the road, literally. Since 1990 Wil Hufton of suburban Flint has been introducing two to thirty persons at a time to the wonders of the rivers and marshlands south of Saginaw through the wilderness excursions he calls **Johnny Panther Quests.** Borrowing the name from an old B-movie character who lived in Florida's swamps, Hufton takes families, couples, and other groups on three- to five-hour treks into the wild, not only explaining the history of the area but the ecology as well. Hufton says that on many trips his passengers see eagles, beavers, muskrats, owls, numerous songbirds, and waterfowl, in the unspoiled natural habitat that covers the thousands of acres of wetlands he's pegged Michigan's Everglades.

Hufton motors his sailboat into the wilds and then floats through the silence. Trips can accommodate ninety-year-olds or younger, more adventurous types who don't mind a portage to see the beauty. He'll even let you off to quietly picnic for a few hours before he returns to pick you up in time for your very own sail into the sunset. You provide your lunch; he provides a cooler, ice, a bag of pistachios, and the silence. A trip to introduce you to the upper Flint River is $80 per couple, plus $30 for each extra person. The Saginaw-area trip is $120 per couple and $50 for each additional passenger. He can also arrange economy accommodations. Call Hufton at (810) 653–3859.

Here's a treat made for kids but loved by folks of all ages. The **Saginaw Children's Zoo,** located in a grove of trees on the city's east side, features twenty-eight species of animals on its eight and a half acres. A special "Contact Area" lets kids meet and pet some of the park's 120 animals. Set your children in the saddle at the pony ride or take them aboard the Ibershoff Special, a miniature-train ride featuring a half-mile loop around the zoo for 75 cents per person. There's also a "Zoovenir Shop," a playground, and food and snack concessions. Admission is $1.50 for anyone thirteen to sixty-four, 75 cents for kids three through twelve, and free for everyone else. The zoo is open from Mother's Day weekend through Labor Day. Hours are 10:00 A.M. to 5:00 P.M. Monday through Saturday and 11:00 A.M. to 6:00 P.M. on Sunday and holidays. To get to the zoo, leave Interstate 675 at the Fifth Street/Sixth Street exit and head south on Washington Avenue approximately 2 miles. The park is on the east side of the street, at 1720 South Washington. For more information call (517) 759–1657.

Located in the middle of Michigan's bean and sugar beet farmland, **Saginaw Valley State University** is the repository of 200 white plaster models of sculptures by the state's (and some say the nation's) foremost artist. In the **Marshall M. Fredericks Sculpture Gallery,** inside the **Arbry Fine Arts Center,** you'll find the models, which are in many respects even more striking than the finished product. Sculptures by Fredericks include the *Spirit of Detroit* bronze outside the City-County Building in downtown Detroit and well-known works across Europe. Donated by the octogenarian artist, who maintains his studio in Royal Oak, north of Detroit, the exhibit draws more than 10,000 visitors annually. Works on display range in size from 1 inch to 28 feet tall. To reach the gallery, exit Interstate 75 at Michigan 84 and turn west. Follow the highway until you see the university sign on the east. The gallery is open Tuesday through Sunday from 1:00 to 5:00 P.M. and is closed on national and university holidays. Admission is free. For more information, call (517) 790–5667.

East Michigan—North

T he northern part of East Michigan drifts from the nation's "beanbasket," which produces more soy, navy, and other bean varieties than any other state, to some of the largest publicly owned tracts of forest land in the nation. The dichotomy amazes even well-traveled Michiganders, who keep coming back, drawn by the diversity. Here are just a few areas to explore.

BAD AXE

Native American rock drawings in Michigan? Yup. In the heart of the state's Thumb, near this city that got its name innocently from an old axe found on the site by early surveyors, are the state's only known prehistoric versions of graffiti, at **Sanilac Petroglyphs State Park.**

Estimated to be more than 1,000 years old, the rock carvings, or petroglyphs, were chiseled into the soft sandstone along the north branch of the Cass River. Kids will marvel at these characters, including the figure of a hunter with a bow and arrow, and others resembling animals. Visitors can also walk a mile-long nature trail through the forested park, where you'll see more marked sites (plan on at least one hour and take along bug repellent). Forty-five-minute guided presentations on the petroglyphs are given in summer. Special events include "Romancing the Stone," a mid-August presentation on Native American folklore. The park is open Wednesday through Sunday from 11:30 A.M. to 4:30 P.M. To find it turn east off Michigan 53 onto Bay City/Forestville Road, travel about 4 miles to Germania Road, and turn south. The park is one-half mile farther, on the west side. It's open Memorial Day through Labor Day. For more information contact the Michigan Historical Museum at (517) 373–3559. Admission is free.

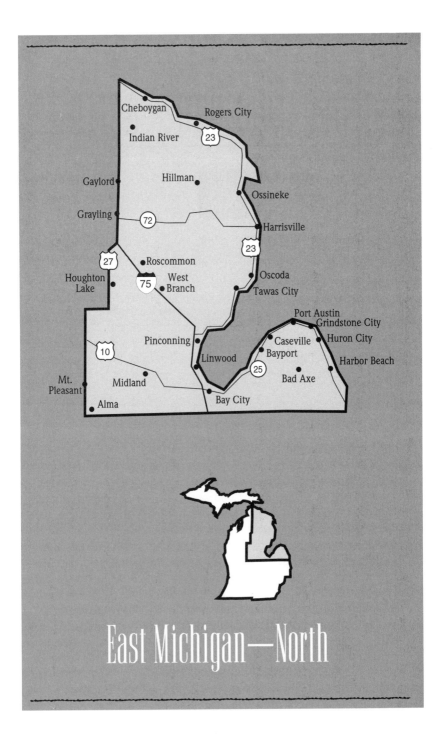

East Michigan—North

HARBOR BEACH

The quiet lakeside resort town of Harbor Beach is home to the **Frank Murphy Museum,** a site dedicated to one of the state's most famous governors. The museum, located inside his birthplace home, tells of Murphy's rise through politics to become governor of the Philippines, then Michigan governor and one hero of the 1937 Flint sit-down strike at General Motors. He won praise when he refused to send in the National Guard to force workers out of the plant, and thus forced GM to recognize the union. The table where that agreement was signed is at the museum. Murphy later went on to become U.S. attorney general and a U.S. Supreme Court justice. The museum is at 142 South Huron Avenue (Michigan 25) and is open from 10:00 A.M. to 6:00 P.M. Wednesday through Sunday from Labor Day to Memorial Day. Admission is by donation. For more information, call (517) 479–9554.

PORT AUSTIN

For one of the best all-around family fun experiences on Lake Huron, sign up for a fishing cruise aboard the ***Miss Port Austin,*** captained by Fred Davis. Twice a day in summer, Davis takes up to twenty anglers aboard his boat moored at the public harbor in this summer vacation town and steers a course toward what many say are the Great Lakes' most delectable prizes: perch.

Using an electronic fish-finder that he'll be happy to show you, Davis maneuvers the *Miss* over schools of perch, a cousin of the walleye that inhabits the sand-and-rock bottom of this stretch of the lake. If you've never fished before and have no equipment, Davis will rent you a rod for the day for $2.00 per person. Then bait up with the minnows he provides, and the rest is up to you. When you feel the first telltale nibble of a fish testing your offering, you'll be on your way to catching a bucketful (the limit is fifty per person). Perch up to 14 inches long are not uncommon. If nothing's doing, Davis will try several spots until the fish start biting. It's a great way to introduce children to the joys of summer on the water, the bird life that typifies the area, and something they can take pleasure from the rest of their lives.

Davis charges $28 per person for trips, with a 20 percent discount for families and seniors on weekdays. From June through August the *Miss Port Austin* leaves from the dock daily at 7:30 A.M. and 2:30 P.M. Call ahead for departures at other times of the spring and fall. You'll need a Michigan-state fishing license (one-day permits are available from area tackle shops; children under age sixteen don't require a license) and a cooler for drinks. Clean your catch at the fish-cleaning station at the dock. Chances are the boat's mate will help you clean for tips. The *Miss Port Austin* ties up at the foot of Michigan 53 in downtown Port

Austin. To reserve a spot on the next voyage, call (517) 738–5271.

HURON CITY

Catch a glimpse of what local life was like in the early twentieth century at the **Huron City Museum,** a restored town on the Lake Huron shore at the tip of Michigan's Thumb. From 1893 until 1938, Huron City was the summer home of William Lyon Phelps, a Yale professor, whose relatives created this unique museum. Before the Phelpses arrived, Huron City was the victim of two horrible fires, in 1871 and 1881, that swept the entire Thumb area's once dense pine forests and destroyed the city's hopes of becoming a major lumbering center like its neighbors to the west.

Each summer families can join guides on one-hour tours of the restored general store, the church where Phelps preached, a log cabin, the town's inn, and the U.S. Lifesaving Station along the beach. The Lifesaving Service was the forerunner of the Coast Guard, and its crew's job was to save passengers and crew from foundering ships along the Thumb's reef-scarred shoreline. From July 1 to Labor Day, the museum is open daily except Tuesday, from 10:00 A.M. to 5:00 P.M. The price of admission depends on which of two tours (the town, the lifesaving station, or both) you'd like to take. Tours of both the town and lifesaving station are $10.00 adults, $3.00 for anyone ten to fifteen years old, and $5.00 for seniors. Children under ten enter free. The last tour of the day is at 4:30 P.M.; the last double tour leaves at 3:30. To reach the museum take Michigan 25 east from Port Austin about 8 miles (it's on the north side of the road). For more information call (517) 428–4123.

GRINDSTONE CITY

To get a mini-lesson in Michigan history and a major lesson in fishing for the "fightingest" fish in the Great Lakes, visit this tiny town that once was the nation's grindstone capital. Located at the very tip of the Thumb, Grindstone City for a century was famous nationwide for producing some of the world's finest grinding stones, which were cut from its limestone quarries and sent to markets around the globe. When other sharpening materials became popular during World War I, the town's two factories closed. Old grindstones ready for export can still be seen lining the roads and driveways in spots. But now Grindstone is known for something else: what may be the best early season **salmon and trout fishing** on the lakes. From its cozy, crescent-shaped harbor, up to a dozen charter boats take anglers on morning and afternoon trips in pursuit of chinook salmon, steelhead (a lake-living rainbow trout), and lake trout.

All gear—and instructions when you hook into a big one—is provided. All you need is a state fishing license (children under sixteen are exempt). The best salmon fishing runs from May to mid-June, and fish over twenty pounds are not uncommon. In summer, lake trout fishing is tops, and by July 20 the salmon return and fishing stays productive through early September. Charters are priced at $250 for a half-day (usually, morning fishing is best, starting at or before sunup) and take up to six persons, so the cost can be split among friends or family members. To get to Grindstone City, take Pointe Aux Barques Road east from Port Austin about 4 miles until it ends, turn north, and watch for the signs directing you to the harbor. For Grindstone City charter boat information, call (517) 738–5500.

CASEVILLE

About 4 miles southwest of Port Austin along Michigan 25 is one of the newest and most picturesque state parks in Michigan. At 565 acres, **Port Crescent** is also one of the last undeveloped stretches of beach along the Thumb. Families can choose from among 181 campsites (try for number 89, a beachside gem nicknamed the "honeymoon site"), roam some of the finest examples of Lake Huron sand dunes in East Michigan, and go for an inland hike on the 6½ miles of nature trails that run along the beach and through the Thumb's surprisingly extensive hardwood forests. The park also includes a fitness trail, fishing access along the Pinnebog River for persons with physical disabilities, and a 3-mile-long beach for daytime use that often is virtually deserted. A few miles south, **Albert E. Sleeper State Park,** one of the oldest and most beautiful in Michigan, preserves 700 acres and features a walkway over Michigan 25 between the campground and the day-use-only beach area. Sleeper has 208 campsites and about 4 miles of nature trails running through the woods. Unsure about camping? Sleeper and Port Crescent also feature mini-cabin rentals by reservation. The cabins are handicapped-accessible and include electricity, bunk beds, and a table and chairs, as well as a grill and fire pit outside. For Port Crescent State Park information, call (517) 738–8663, and for Sleeper State Park, (517) 856–4411.

BAY PORT

Just a few miles east is another Thumb icon, the **Bay Port Fish Company.** Chances are better than average that eighty-one-year-old former owner Henry Englehard will be holding forth. Englehard, who netted the bay for fifty-one years, will greet you with a smile and bend your ear if you let him with bay tales, including how a stand he started selling fish sandwiches from in front of his house evolved into the **Bay Port Fish Sandwich Festival,** held annually the first full weekend in August. More than 8,000 fish sandwiches are sold during the two-day townwide celebration. You can also pick up those Great Lakes delicacies, fresh perch and smoked or fresh whitefish, at Bay Port Fish. For information on the festival, call (517) 656–7298, and on the Bay Port Fish Company, (517) 656–2131.

BAY CITY

This former rip-roaring lumber town has settled down a bit from when bars along the Saginaw River held trapdoors waiting for unsuspecting lumberjacks who'd just gotten paid and had too much to drink, but the excitement has shifted to more legitimate action. Bay City, with its scores of Victorian-era buildings and quaint downtown, is the setting for some of the region's best special events, recreational activities, and shopping.

On the river's east side, stock up on the PB part of PB&J sandwiches at **St. Laurent's Nut House,** at 1101 North Water, where all-natural, low-sodium, smooth, and crunchy peanut butter is sold in tubs of up to five pounds. While the kids are inside picking out some penny candies, antiques fans can hop kitty-corner across the street, to the **Bay City Antiques Center,** 1010 Water, which has more than a hundred vendors and an antique soda fountain where you can wet your whistle with an old-fashioned malt or phosphate.

Just to the south is **Wenonah Park,** a site for numerous summer festivals, concerts, and sporting events, including the **Bay City River Roar** boat races, held the third weekend of June, and the **Fourth of July fireworks,** billed as the largest show in the region. Don't forget to walk the 2-mile-long waterfront boardwalk, the **Riverwalk,** on the river's west bank, which has markers along the way that tell of the city's history.

Six miles north on the west side is **Bay City State Park,** offering camping. Swimming, however, is somewhat hampered by beached zebra mussels, brought in from Europe aboard a passing ship and now a Great Lakes nuisance and threat. The beach is now near the park store. Nearby is the **Jennison Nature Center,** with 5 miles of nature trails, including one with braille signs and another leading to a tower looking over **Tobico Marsh.** For more on Bay City events and activities, call the Bay Area Convention and Visitors Bureau at (517) 893-4567, or (800) 424–5114. St. Laurent's Nut House is open from 9:00 A.M. to 9:00 P.M. Monday through Saturday and from 11:00 A.M. to 5:00 P.M. on Sunday; call (517) 893–7522. The antiques market is open from 10:00 A.M. to 5:00 P.M. Monday through Thursday, and on Saturday, from 10:00 A.M.

BILL'S TOP FAMILY ADVENTURES IN EAST MICHIGAN—NORTH

1. Fishing aboard the *Miss Port Austin,* Port Austin
2. Deer Acres, Pinconning
3. Corsair Ski Area, Tawas City/East Tawas
4. North and South Higgings Lake State Parks, Roscommon
5. Indian River Catholic Shrine, Indian River

to 8:00 P.M. on Friday, and from noon to 5:00 P.M. on Sunday; call (517) 893–1116. Contact Bay City State Park at (517) 684–3020. To reach the downtown area from Interstate 75, get off at Business Interstate 75 east, which becomes Michigan 25. Continue east across the Saginaw River, turn north on Saginaw, then west, toward the river, on Fourth. Water Street is the next intersection. To reach Bay City State Park, exit Interstate 75 at Beaver Road (exit 168) and drive east 5 miles.

MIDLAND

The city that aspirin built has lots to offer the family, from plant tours to the arts to nature study. When your job or the kids seem too much to handle and you reach for the aspirin bottle, chances are good that the product originated at Midland's giant **Dow Chemical Company.** On a 2 ½-hour tour of the city's major employer, visitors can see how some of the more than 1,000 Dow products are made, including the raw ingredients for almost all the aspirin made in this country, as well as Saran Wrap. The company was founded by Dr. Herbert H. Dow in 1890 to begin extracting bromine and chlorine, plus chemicals as innocuous as Epsom salts, from the area's brine wells. At the end of your tour, you'll get a free roll of the plastic wrap that started it all. Tours take place Mondays at 9:30 A.M. To reach the plant, get off exit U.S. 10 at the Business U.S. 10 exit, follow it to Bayliss Street, and turn south onto Bayliss. The Dow Visitor Center is at the corner of Bayliss and Lyon. Make tour reservations by calling the center at (517) 636–8659.

At the **Chippewa Nature Center,** activities focus on humankind's inter-action with the planet. One of its most popular events is the Maple Sugaring

Weekend, which begins on the third Saturday in March. Families can tour the 1,000-acre center with a naturalist and follow the process that turns watery sugar-maple sap into thick, luscious syrup in the center's Sugar Shack. Other perfect family activities include nature walks through the center's 12 miles of trails, exploring a restored 1870s farm and log school, and naturalist-led programs such as insect, reptile, and flower identification in summer. The nature center is at 400 South Badour Road. To reach it take the Business U.S. 10 exit off U.S. 10, turn south onto Cronkrigt, and then go north on St. Charles, the first street past the Tittabawassee. Watch for the sign at the "Y" in the road, drive about 3 miles on farther, and you'll see the entrance. Admission is by donation. The center is open Monday through Friday from 8:00 A.M. to 5:00 P.M., Saturday from 9:00 A.M. to 5:00 P.M., and Sunday and most holidays from 1:00 to 5:00 P.M. Call (517) 631–0830 to hear about the latest exhibits.

ALMA

Each Memorial Day weekend this small town, whose largest draw the rest of the year is its private Alma College, welcomes up to 80,000 visitors who either have a touch of Scotch brogue in their background or wish they did. At the annual **Alma Highland Festival and Games,** you can show your kids that yes, Scotsmen really do wear kilts, even when they compete in contests such as the caber and stone toss—old training techniques dating from the times when the English would not let the Scots have weapons. In these contests of strength and skill, competitors see how far they can flip a piece of wood the size of a telephone pole, and how far they can push a heavy chunk of rock (sizes vary according to class). Scottish-style food, dancing demonstrations and contests, and lots of bagpipe music prevail the entire weekend, as does other fun, including sheep herding demonstrations, and arts-and-crafts sales. Alma is north of Lansing along U.S. 27. To get to the festival area, take the Alma exit downtown to the Alma College campus. Festival hours are 9:00 a.m to 5:00 P.M. on both Saturday and Sunday. Admission is $8.00 for teens and adults, $5.00 for children age six through twelve and seniors over sixty-two; children five and under are free. For more information on the event and other Alma activities, call the area chamber of commerce at (517) 463–5525.

MOUNT PLEASANT

Just up the road from Alma, near the site of one of Michigan's early oil-and-gas discoveries and the geographical center of the state, is Mount Pleasant. Home to Central Michigan University, the city puts on lots of different faces throughout the year. Family-oriented events include the **Mount Pleasant Summer Festival,** on the second weekend in June, with fun such as a carnival and fireworks and music all day. The **Co-Expo World Championship Rodeo** is held the third weekend in June. Riders and cowpokes from across North America come to compete and rack up points in hopes of being recognized as the world's best in events from bull riding to barrel racing. The rodeo takes place at the Isabella County Fairgrounds, reached by taking the Michigan 20 exit west off U.S. 27 and then going west on Pickard to Mission; turn north onto Mission, then west onto Old Mission, which leads to the grounds. For more information on area events and attractions, call the Mount Pleasant/Isabella County Convention and Visitors Bureau at (517) 772–4433 or (800) 772–4433.

LINWOOD

In Linwood, the **Williams Cheese Company,** at 998 North Huron Road (Michigan 13), south of Deer Acres, sells its own brand of Pinconning cheese, a softer version of Colby, prepared at its cheese-making plant. Hours at the retail store are 8:00 A.M. to 5:00 P.M. on Saturday and Monday through Thursday, 8:00 A.M. to 7:00 P.M. on Friday, and 10:00 A.M. to 4:00 P.M. on Sunday; call (517) 697–4492.

PINCONNING

This East Michigan town may be nicknamed Michigan's cheese capital because its factories produce the cheddarlike Pinconning cheese, but there's nothing cheesy about **Deer Acres,** five minutes to the south. Since 1959 this attraction, painted a bright chartreuse and located on the east side of Michigan 13, has attracted an average of 40,000 families each summer. Kids love to hand-feed the herds of deer—and the deer love the attention, too. They've learned to come running when they hear the sound of the deer food dispensers clicking all over the park. In Story Book Village, kids can meet all their favorite Mother Goose and other storybook characters, like Peter Pumpkin and Jack, the beanstalk-climbing giant-killer. Pack a lunch and use the grills and picnic tables, or head for the snack shop. Five amusement rides include a narrated trip past storybook characters and life-size models of animals depicting how and where they live in the wild, and a narrated ½-mile-long minitrain excursion. Deer Acres is reached from Interstate 75 by taking exit 164 at Kawkawlin and going north on Michigan 13 for about fifteen minutes. It's open daily May 15 through Labor Day, from 9:00 A.M. to 7:00 P.M., and then, until October 15, on weekends only, from 10:00 A.M. to 6:00 P.M. Admission is $6.75 for teens and adults, $4.75 for children ages three to twelve, and $5.75 for seniors. Call (517) 879–2849 for more information.

TAWAS CITY/EAST TAWAS

You'd expect a vacation area like this to have the usual tourist draws, like minigolf and go-carts, but your family will be "amazed," literally, at **Maze of the Planets,** one of the state's first fun and educational English-style mazes. In fact, it was built by English maze architects. But unlike traditional English hedge mazes, this one takes you along 3,500 feet of pathways defined by 652 7-foot-high wooden walls and four bridges. The goal is to reach the 16-foot-tall tower and another "colour maze" in the center shaped like Saturn. On the way, kids search for the nine planets hidden throughout the maze. Armed with a quiz card, they find answers to the questions posted at each planet. It's all handicapped-accessible, and the pattern always changes. Cost is $4.00 per person. The maze is open from 10:00 A.M. to 10:00 P.M. daily from Memorial Day to Labor Day and on weekends in fall. It's at 1760 North U.S. 23, about 4 miles north of East Tawas's downtown; call (517) 362–2111.

When winter comes to the dense Huron National Forest, about 6 miles outside the twin cities of Tawas City/East Tawas, it signals an entirely new season of family fun at the **Corsair Ski Area.** Some 35 miles of trails on both sides of Monument Road beckon cross-country ski enthusiasts of all ability levels to the series of looping courses that always begin and end at the three large parking areas. Beginners can take always-groomed, mostly flat trails that wind through the dense woods around trout-filled Silver Creek, while intermediates and advanced types can be challenged by hilly terrain with some mean curves thrown in. Gary Nelke, owner of East Tawas's Nordic Sports shop, can outfit your family in cross-country skis and shoes and will start you off with an in-store lesson if you ask. Nordic Sports is at 218 West Bay Street in East Tawas. Reach him for equipment reservations and trail conditions at (517) 362–2001.

Each February you can combine skiing with **Perchville, USA,** the festival on the ice at East Tawas. Some 15,000 persons stroll about for fun, and many go after the schools of perch swimming underneath the bay ice. One of the festival's most amusing events takes place near the state's longest wooden dock. A few hardy and normally responsible souls, who might have been cooped up in their cabins a mite too long, dive into frigid Lake Huron through a hole chopped in the ice. Other events include frozen softball and children's games, plus a Friday-night, all-you-can-eat perch dinner.

In summer take the family to the beach at **Tawas Point State Park,** about 4 miles north of the cities, where there's also a working lighthouse. The cities are along U.S. 23. For more information call the Tawas Area Chamber of Commerce at (800) 55–TAWAS, or (517) 362–8643.

OSCODA

Only 15 miles up the road is the beachside town of Oscoda, where more summer fun awaits. Charter a boat at the mouth of the **Au Sable River** and fish Lake Huron for salmon and trout, or rent a canoe and take the family on a paddle tour of the gentle lower river. Head west out of Oscoda by turning from U.S. 23 onto the **Au Sable River Road,** a designated scenic highway through the **Huron National Forest,** where three more attractions await. In fall at **Foote Dam,** watch as chinook salmon make their spawning runs up the river as anglers try to catch them. The dam is located at Foote Site Village, about 6 miles west of Oscoda. Just follow the signs.

Above the dam, climb aboard an authentic paddle wheeler for a lazy trip through the impoundment on the *Au Sable River Queen.* The 19-mile narrated trips run about two hours. Follow Captain Bill Norris's running commentary about the river's history and wildlife. The area is especially beautiful and popular in fall (reservations are required for fall trips). Cost of the trip is $8.25 for teens and adults (for the fall-color tours, the price rises to $11.00) and $4.00 ($5.25 in fall) for children ages five to twelve; there's also a 10 percent discount for seniors except during fall-color season. The boats run from Memorial Day weekend through the third weekend in October. Call (517) 739–7351 for details.

After your cruise enjoy the rest of the scenic byway. At **Lumberman's Monument,** 16 miles west of Oscoda, a 14-foot-high bronze sculpture depicts a riverman, a land "timber cruiser" perusing a map, and a woodsman with an ax and crosscut saw—a scene dedicated to Michigan's lumbering heyday, 1840 to 1890. Lumberjacks like these helped build the nation, make some men millionaires, and, at the same time, destroy the virgin pine forests. A visitors center that's open from 10:00 A.M. to 7:00 P.M. mid-April through October explains the story. The grounds are open from 6:00 A.M. to 10:00 P.M. daily year-round. Call (517) 362–8961 for information. Walk the 260 steps down the edge of Cook Dam Pond, or enjoy the barrier-free walk and deck overlooking the scene from the high banks above. About 1 mile farther west, crossed canoe paddles over the river far below mark the **Canoeist's Memorial,** and a mile later kids will love to take the 200-plus steps down the high banks to **Iargo Springs,** a naturally flowing well that Native Americans once used. The water flows at a near-constant temperature in the midfifties. Both sites are open year-round. For more information on byway attractions, call (800) 821–6263, (517) 362–4477, or (517) 739–0728.

The Lumberman's Monument, located in Oscoda, pays tribute to the lumberjacks that made Michigan's lumber industry thrive during the second half of the 1800s. (Photo by Robert Brodbeck)

WEST BRANCH

One of Michigan's newest outlet malls is the **Tanger Factory Outlet Mall**, just off Interstate 75 at exit 212. Thirty stores are there to keep families busy hunting for the best bargains, including Ralph Lauren and Coach. Hours most of the year are 10:00 A.M. to 9:00 P.M. Monday through Saturday and 11:00

A.M. to 7:00 P.M. on Sunday. From January through the end of March, the stores are open from 10:00 A.M. to 6:00 P.M. Monday through Thursday, from 10:00 A.M. to 9:00 P.M. on Friday and Saturday, and from noon to 6:00 P.M. on Sunday. For information call (517) 345–4437.

HOUGHTON LAKE

About ninety minutes west of the Oscoda-Tawas area, via Michigan 55 from Tawas City, is Houghton Lake. With more than thirty-one square miles of surface, it's Michigan's largest inland lake. Along its edges the towns of Houghton Lake and Prudenville have been family vacation destinations for decades, and resorts, motels, and cottages line the shoreline. There are plenty of things to do when you're not at the beach, too, especially in Houghton Lake. Go-cart rides, miniature and full-size golf, and, of course, fishing for the lake's walleye and panfish are just some.

Be sure to take in a movie in what is perhaps Michigan's most unusual movie theater. **The Pines** has been a handsome local landmark since 1941. It's Michigan's only movie house constructed completely of western Douglas fir logs. Inside the lobby are examples of Michigan wildlife, including deer, ducks, and pheasant, and movie buffs will find such memorabilia as autographed posters of Hollywood star Charlton Heston, whose family has a cottage in nearby St. Helen and who often visited the theater. Still part of the auditorium's 500 seats are "love seats" that can fit two cuddlers. The Pines is open in winter, and there are two shows nightly from Memorial Day weekend through Labor Day. The theater is at 4673 West Houghton Lake Road (Michigan 55). Tickets are $5.00 for adults and $3.00 for children. Call (517) 366–9226 for show times.

Down the street in Houghton Lake, the rhythmic sounds of drums and ancient chants once again echo each summer as they have for the last forty years at **Zubler's craft store.** Every Thursday from June through August, Native Americans from the Swan Creek and Black River bands of Chippewa and Odawa travel from the Mount Pleasant area to demonstrate Native American dances and crafts inside a circle of permanent tepees next to the store. Often, dancers will coax young audience members to join in. Native American storytelling includes tales of the wise coyote and how ducks got their quacks. There are crafts for sale and more inside Zubler's, which specializes in Southwest Indian and Cherokee items. Zubler's is at 3282 West Houghton Lake Drive (Michigan 55). For schedule updates call (517) 366–5691.

The fun doesn't stop in winter, either. Snow sculptures, ice-fishing contests, snowmobiling, and a frosty parade make up **Tip-Up-Town,** the annual winter carnival that draws upwards of 60,000 persons during the last two full weekends in January. It's named for a particular type of ice-fishing rod that tips up when a fish bites and has been a winter fixture here since 1950. For more information on the area, including a cottage-and-resort guide, call the Houghton Lake Chamber of Commerce at (517) 366–5644 or (800) 248–LAKE.

ROSCOMMON

Consistently ranked in Michigan reader polls as having the favorite inland lake beach, **North and South Higgins Lake State Parks** are located on a body of water that members of the National Geographic Society once voted the world's sixth most beautiful.

Higgins Lake South is especially well liked by families with young children, as knee-high kids can wade on its shelf of hard sand and rolling bars for up to 700 feet out before mom and dad have to worry too much about the depth. Along with 512 modern campsites and plenty of wooded picnic space, there are cross-country ski and hiking trails.

Higgins Lake North has as many family-friendly attributes, too, and it's just across the street from an attraction worth a trip in itself. **The CCC Museum** is a replica of a Civilian Conservation Corps barracks that honors the thousands who served in the CCC during the Depression. From 1933 to 1942 unemployed single men between seventeen and twenty-three found work reforesting the north, refurbishing state parks, and constructing roads and bridges. The building shows how they lived and labored in 123 camps scattered around the state. Hours are 10:00 A.M. to 6:00 P.M. from June 13 through Labor Day and by appointment. To reach the museum and both parks, exit Interstate 75 at Roscommon Road; head south for Higgins Lake South, or west on Roscommon Road to Higgins Lake North and the museum. For museum information call (517) 373–3559, and for park information call the south unit at (517) 821–6374; the north unit at (517) 821–6125.

In downtown Roscommon you can also take the family **canoeing** along the South Branch of the Au Sable River. This branch, which joins the main stream about 20 miles north by water, is one of the most scenic, as much of it flows through the **Mason Wilderness Tract,** a 16-mile stretch of pristine natural beauty. Wildlife from deer to bald eagles and coyotes can be seen along its banks. Liveries are located in and near Roscommon; call the chamber of commerce at (517) 275–8760 for a list. To reach downtown take exit 239 off Interstate 75 and turn north.

GRAYLING

Michigan is filled with beautiful floatable rivers, but probably the best, most family-fun-oriented, and certainly the most popular in East Michigan is the upper Au Sable River, which flows through this former lumber town. You can canoe the main stream from any of several liveries in downtown Grayling. Each offers relaxing float trips as short as two hours and as lengthy as week-long paddles to the mouth of the Au Sable in Oscoda.

You can become a part of Michigan floating history while fishing, bird-watching, or just enjoying the ripple of water and quiet of the day by heading out in an authentic **Au Sable River Drift Boat.** They've been part of the river scene here for more than a hundred years, first as supply craft. Guides in the area include Bob Andrus, a Grayling schoolteacher in fall and winter. He and others will take you on a daylong, half-day, or night float on the river. Usually, the riverboats are 20 to 24 feet long and take one or two persons plus guide. Passengers sit forward and the guide steers from the stern. Part of the fun can be a shore lunch over a wood fire. Besides trout, you'll probably see beavers, deer, ducks, muskrat, and an assortment of birds that might include herons and bald eagles. The cost of a float trip is about $275. For a list of guides, call the Grayling Chamber of Commerce at (517) 348–2921.

There are scores of motels in the Grayling area, but unique is **Gates Au Sable Lodge,** nestled by the river 6 miles east of the city. A stay at the Gates place will introduce you to the quiet joys of trout fishing up close. With sixteen rooms renting for reasonable prices (about $70 for a two-bed room), you'll get a large space with a picture window view of the river through the trees that cover the property. There's a restaurant and fly shop. If you're a new angler, come to the fly-fishing workshop held each spring; or arrange a float with one of the lodge's guides. Then take the kids down to the"bread hole" under a willow over the river, where huge trout gulp crusts. To reach the lodge, take exit 254 off northbound Interstate 75 and turn east on Michigan 72; follow it to Stephan Bridge Road and turn north. The lodge is at the bridge. For reservation information call (517) 348–8462.

Along the Au Sable's tiny East Branch, take the kids to feed trout from fingerling size to several pounds at the **Grayling Fish Hatchery.** Dating from 1914, the state hatchery was closed for production of fish in the 1960s. It reopened as a tourist attraction in 1983. Currently, eleven ponds raise up to 45,000 trout—for fishing by the inch in a designated area, to supply a local trout farm, and to delight kids. The hatchery is on North Down River Road. Off

Interstate 75, take Exit 254, follow Interstate 75 Business Loop through town, and turn north at the Clark gasoline station; then follow the signs. Admission is $1.00 for adults and 50 cents for children ages five to seventeen. The hatchery is open daily Memorial Day to Labor Day between 10:00 A.M. and 6:00 P.M. For information call (517) 348–9266.

Afterward, head to the **Stevens Family Circle** restaurant at 231 Michigan Avenue in downtown Grayling. Rolls, soups, salads, and sandwiches are outshone by the old-fashioned soda fountain for phosphates, coolers, cones, and malteds. The restaurant is not open Sundays. For information call (517) 348–2111.

Six miles north of Grayling, you'll see almost all that remains of the giants that once covered nearly all of Michigan. In **Hartwick Pines State Park,** donated to the state by the wife of a local lumberman, visitors can walk miles of trails covered by a canopy of huge white pines and hemlocks that block so much sunlight hardly any vegetation grows on the forest floor. A restored logging camp, complete with a "big wheel" (which was used to haul logs out of the forest), a bunkhouse, and a dining room, is set deep in the woods. In summer the camp comes alive three times a year as living-history portrayals explain what logging life was like in the old days. Events take place during Woodshavings and Sawdust Days in July and Black Iron Days in August. There's a campground for summer use, mountain-biking trails, and cross-country skiing in winter. To get to the park, take Interstate 75 exit 264 and drive about 2 miles east on Michigan 93. For information call (517) 348–7068.

HARRISVILLE

If you're looking for a serene, family-oriented resort that ranks among the top in the state, try **Big Paw,** a pleasant enclave hidden behind a green cedar curtain along U.S. 23, 1½ miles north of this vacation town. Big Paw operates on a modified American plan (breakfast and dinner are included), so your stay might require a mite more cash than other places, but no one has to cook. Choose from three cottages plus the Four Paws Lodge, a quartet of cabinlike cedar dens, each with a fieldstone fireplace and fronting on a quarter-mile of secluded Lake Huron sugary sand. A tennis court and hiking trails let guests work up an appetite for the weekly hot-dog roast on the beach. Owners Ron and Nancy Yokum will also arrange salmon-fishing charters—and there's cable TV for the kids, too. For reservation information call (517) 724–6326.

GAYLORD/HILLMAN

In fall the distinctive bugling of **Michigan's elk herd** can be heard for miles through the **Pigeon River State Forest** between Gaylord and Hillman. The herd of more than 1,000, largest east of the Mississippi, inhabit some of the wildest forest in Lower Michigan. In summer some of the best places to spot them are in one of several clearings they're known to frequent especially at dusk. In winter there's a more romantic way, near Hillman. Jack Matthias, who owns **Thunder Bay Golf Resort,** takes up to twenty persons on sleigh rides (hay rides in fall) through the countryside to elk habitat in the **Mackinaw State Forest.** Afterward, you'll enjoy a five-course champagne dinner. For information on the ride and the resort, call (800) 729–9375 or (517) 742–4502.

Gaylord also is home to the annual **Alpenfest.** Swiss-inspired traditions such as the burning of the Boogg—where residents place all their troubles on pieces of paper and send them up in smoke—together with parades and the world's largest coffee break are part of the fun in mid-July. Gaylord is along Interstate 75 about 20 miles north of Grayling. Hillman is east of Gaylord along Michigan 32. For elk viewing and Alpenfest information, contact the Gaylord Area Convention and Tourism Bureau at (800) 345–8621, or (517) 732–4000.

INDIAN RIVER

Rent a pontoon boat and float along all or part of Michigan's unknown canal, the **Inland Waterway.** This 68-mile, partly artificial, partly natural cut through the tip-of-Michigan's "mitt" takes you to some of the state's largest inland lakes and through two locks. Travelers can begin in Indian River and head all the way to Cheboygan on Lake Huron or to Crooked Lake, a few miles from Lake Michigan. While the waterway doesn't connect to the big lake, you can rent a trailer from a local marina to take your craft there. For rental information contact the Indian River Chamber of Commerce at (616) 238–9325.

Before leaving the area, be sure to see the **Cross in the Woods at the Indian River Catholic Shrine,** overlooking Burt Lake, one of the water bodies linked by the canal. Created by Michigan sculptor Marshall Fredericks, the world's largest crucifix is mounted on a 55-foot-high redwood cross and looks out over one of the state's most pastoral settings, near **Burt Lake State Park.** It's the focal point of a thirteen-acre outdoor Catholic church that draws worshipers in summer for daily masses. Visitors of all faiths can walk the shrine's paths through the woods. A gift shop features religious articles, and in the

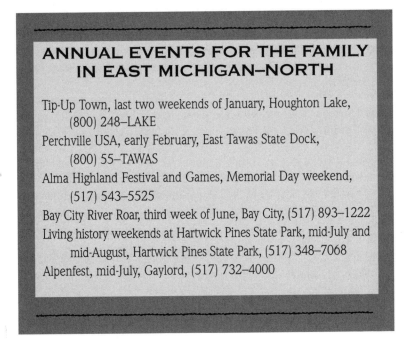

**ANNUAL EVENTS FOR THE FAMILY
IN EAST MICHIGAN—NORTH**

Tip-Up Town, last two weekends of January, Houghton Lake,
    (800) 248–LAKE
Perchville USA, early February, East Tawas State Dock,
    (800) 55–TAWAS
Alma Highland Festival and Games, Memorial Day weekend,
    (517) 543–5525
Bay City River Roar, third week of June, Bay City, (517) 893–1222
Living history weekends at Hartwick Pines State Park, mid-July and
    mid-August, Hartwick Pines State Park, (517) 348–7068
Alpenfest, mid-July, Gaylord, (517) 732–4000

lower level there's a museum featuring more than 500 dolls dressed in nun and priest habits from nearly every Catholic order. To get to the shrine, exit Interstate 75 at Indian River (exit 310) and follow the signs along Michigan 68. For information call (616) 238–8973.

OSSINEKE

A bit to the east is a low-key tourist destination that has attracted families to its wooded setting for almost half a century. **Dinosaur Gardens Prehistorical Zoo** has been entertaining and educating youngsters since 1938. It took original owner Paul Domke thirty-eight years to sculpt the twenty-six life-size dinos set amid the pines and hardwood forest that line the winding Devil River. Story boards at each exhibit tell visitors what scientists believe the lives of these magnificently fearsome animals were like. In one scene a towering tyrannosaur battles a horned triceratops, and in another an animal roars in frustration after being trapped in a lake of tar. A gift shop sells souvenirs, including plastic dinosaur models. Dinosaur Gardens is at 11160 U.S. 23 and is open 9:00 A.M.

to 6:00 P.M. daily from Memorial Day to Labor Day. Admission is $3.00 for adults and teens, $2.00 for children ages six through twelve, and $1.00 for kids five and under. Call (517) 471–5477 for more information.

ROGERS CITY

While other vacationers head to Michigan's west coast for everything from huge hotels to condoplexes, northeastern Michigan's main attraction is the lack of the same. Just plenty of natural things to help you relax and keep you busy at the same time. One such area surrounds this city. The tiny town doesn't look like much, just another spot to gas up and go. But look again.

If there'd been no Rogers City, you might not have the car you drive. A few miles south, just off U.S. 23, is the world's largest quarry for limestone, one of the principal elements in steelmaking. Look out from **Quarry View** into a hole more than 3 miles long and 2 miles wide. At **Harbor View,** watch giant Great Lakes freighters pulling up to the docks to load before heading for mills in Indiana, Ohio, and Detroit. Take the kids into the wheelhouse of the retired freighter *Calcite.* More on the quarry operations, the town's early lumbering days, and subsequent events, including the 1958 sinking of the freighter *Carl D. Bradley,* which was crewed by several local residents, is at the **Presque Isle County Historical Museum,** 176 North Michigan, in town. It's open weekdays noon to 4:00 P.M. from June through October. Admission is free. Call (517) 734–4121 for more information.

A few miles to the south, on a spit of land between Grand Lake and Lake Huron, is the **Old Presque Isle Lighthouse Museum.** Built in 1840, it is filled with period antiques—and some say it's haunted by a former lightkeeper. The museum is open from 9:00 A.M. to 7:00 P.M. daily from May 1 to October 15. To get there, turn east off U.S. 23 at County Road 638 (East Grand Lake Road), travel past two stop signs, and turn right onto Grand Lake Road. Follow it about 9 miles and you'll see the lighthouse on the right-hand side. Admission is $1.50 for adults and teens, and 50 cents for children six to twelve. Call (517) 595–2787 or (517) 595–2706 for more information.

Head west of Rogers City along Michigan 68 to reach **Ocqueoc** *(ock-kee-ock)* **Falls,** largest in the Lower Peninsula. A park is located at the site. Rogers City also has become a hot spot for **salmon fishing** and is touted by some as the best in the state in mid- to late summer. For information about charter boats and lodging, which ranges from cottages to motels, call (517) 734–2535 or (800) 622–4148.

CHEBOYGAN

Only 20 or so miles from the top of the Lower Peninsula is Cheboygan, one of whose claims to fame is that it's the home port of the **coast guard icebreaker** *Mackinaw*. When the vessel is in port along the Cheboygan River, it's most always open for tours. Call the Cheboygan Area Tourist Bureau at (616) 627–7183 for more information on its operations.

Other attractions here include fine local theater at the 1877 **Cheboygan Opera House,** located at 403 North Huron. Guided tours of the opera house are also available. Plays are performed during November. Phone (616) 627–5432 for more information. The **Cheboygan County Historical Museum** is in the former county sheriff's home, which doubled as a jail from 1882 to 1969 and still has eight cells. Admission is $2.00 for adults and $1.00 for primary- and secondary-school students. The museum is at Huron and Court streets, one block west of Main Street. Hours are 1:00 to 4:00 P.M. Monday through Friday from June 15 to September 15. Call (616) 627–5448 or 627–9597 for more information.

West Michigan—South

F ruit orchards, sandy beaches, marinas, artist colonies, cities celebrating their ethnic heritage—West Michigan has a wealth of activities, spread from the Indiana state line to one of the state's most popular tourist destinations, Mackinaw City. The southern portion of this region is a great place to start your explorations.

BRIDGMAN

Covering more than 2½ miles of beautiful Lake Michigan shore near the small town of Bridgman, **Warren Dunes State Park** has become one of the state's most popular, welcoming more than one million visitors annually. Encompassing 1,507 acres, the park is known for its continually changing sand dunes that greet motorists as soon as they turn onto the entrance road. For many coming from Indiana or Illinois, it's the first glimpse of the magnificent Lake Michigan sand shore that stretches nearly the length of West Michigan.

Walk the beach of fine silica sand and tell your kids to shuffle through it. It literally squeaks. Head into the dunes along 6 miles of marked hiking trails. Watch for the tops of trees long ago covered by the shifting sands. There are nearly 200 modern campsites, as well as three cabins to rent. Parts of the park are heavily wooded, but there are hundreds of acres of high sand dunes, too. The park is open year-round. To reach it, take exit 16 off Interstate 94 and go 2 miles south. Day-use entry is by state-issued vehicle permit ($4.00 for a single day or $20.00 annually). For more information call (616) 426–4013.

Nearby is the **Cook Energy Information Center,** built next to the Cook Nuclear Plant, one of the Midwest's largest such facilities, serving seven states. The center explores the world of energy, electricity, and nuclear power. Included

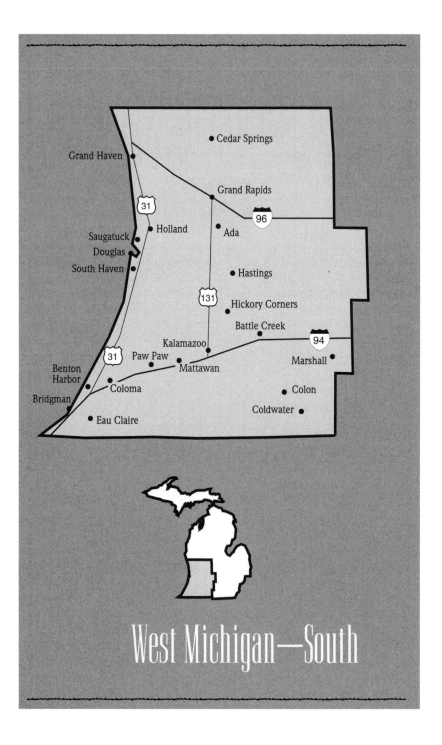

Cedar Springs

Grand Haven

31

Grand Rapids

96

Saugatuck
Douglas
South Haven

Holland

Ada

Hastings

131

Hickory Corners

Battle Creek

Kalamazoo

94

Benton
Harbor

31

Paw Paw

Marshall

Mattawan

Bridgman

Coloma

Colon

Coldwater

Eau Claire

West Michigan—South

in the exhibits are three theaters, where presentations tell about the future of energy and homes. Also on display is an explanation of how power is produced by nuclear fission next door. The center is used for community arts-and-crafts shows, too. It is at 1 Cook Place. Reach it by leaving Interstate 94 at exit 16, going north onto Red Arrow Highway, and driving about 3½ miles. Admission is free. For information on upcoming programs, call (616) 465–6101.

EAU CLAIRE

Each July people gather here for a what? You heard right. **Eau Claire's Tree-Mendus Fruit Farm** is home to the **International Cherry Pit–Spitting Championship.** This contest does the one your kids may have had with their friends one better. At their 500-acre orchard in the heart of the area's fruit belt, owners Herbert and Liz Teichman have cooked up an annual event that has put them on the map nationwide. The best lips and mouths converge each year to see who can spit a pit the farthest. The world-record spit was set in 1988 and still stands at 72 feet, 7 inches. Before and after the contest, tour the orchards to learn how the fruit has evolved. You'll pass ancient types of trees, dwarfs, and exotic hybrids. Tours by reservation are offered from May to November. A store also sells preserves and other items. The contest takes place on the first Saturday in July at 10:00 A.M. The orchard is open from 10:00 A.M. to 6:00 P.M. It's located at 9351 Eureka Road and is reached by taking exit 29 off Interstate 94 and heading east on Meadowbrook Road; turn south onto Michigan 140 and go about 6 miles to Eureka, then head east 1 mile to the orchard. For more information call (616) 782–7101.

COLON

If you say a visit to this tiny town is truly magical, you're right. Faster than you can say "abracadabra," the kids and the rest of the family can disappear inside the **Abbott Magic Company** to seek out items for Halloween and tricks to dazzle their friends back home. Lacquered Chinese boxes, black top hats, magic wands, rubber chickens, and fake raccoons are among the more than 2,000 products Abbott sells to magicians around the globe, supporting Colon's claim that it's the "Magic Capital of the World." Each year on the first weekend in August, thousands of professional and amateur magicians converge on the town to take part in the **Magic Get-Together.** For four days they pay homage to the memory of Harry Blackstone Sr., the former Colon resident who became world-famous for his illusions. Daily magic shows at the company's showroom in the afternoons and at Colon High School in the evenings are open to the public. Cost is about $3.00 for the showroom presentations and $12.00 ($9.00 for children six through twelve) for evening shows. Colon is 16 miles west of Coldwater along Michigan 86. The Abbott Magic Company is at 124 St. Joseph, a block west of Michigan 86. Its retail store hours are 8:00 A.M. to 5:00 P.M. Monday through Friday and 8:00 A.M. to 4:00 P.M. on Saturday. For more information on the store and the festival, call (616) 432–3235.

COLOMA

If you can't make it to Colon in time for Halloween, head to this town along busy Interstate 94. What began as a small grocery here is now one of the Midwest's most popular day attractions for would-be ghosts, goblins, and lovers of all things that go bump in the night.

Owner Paul Friday of **Farmer Friday's** has concocted a magical fanta-syland where, following a buffet turkey dinner, if you wish, you can wander into his **Haunted Barn**—the one with the 24-foot-tall, steaming "mad spider" crawling on its roof—to marvel at the electronic wonders Friday, nicknamed Mr. Halloween, and his employees have dreamed up. On the second floor browse through more than 1,000 costumes and rubber masks. Among the panoply you'll find Fred Flintstone and Barney Rubble, Bill Clinton and Ross Perot. There's even a spooky twelve-hole indoor golf course. As Halloween nears, employees dress up in scary costumes and don nicknames to match. Farmer Friday's is off exit 39 on Interstate 94. The turkey buffet is $4.99 ($5.99 on Sunday), with special children's rates of $1.00 plus 30 cents for each year of age up to ten. Admission to the haunted barn is $5.00 ($3.50 for children ten and under) and the golf course costs $2.50. For more information call (616) 468–5512.

COLDWATER

Besides its great Victorian shopping district, this town on the western edge of the Irish Hills includes the **Tibbits Opera House,** at 14 Hanchett Street, south of U.S. 12. Opened in 1882, it still presents summer stock June through August and offers free theater tours from 9:00 A.M. to 6:00 P.M. Monday through Friday. For reservation information call (517) 278–6029.

MARSHALL

To the north along Interstate 69 is the historic town of Marshall. The first weekend after Labor Day brings the annual **Marshall Historic Home Tour,** featuring a close-up look at more than fifteen houses and other buildings in the

BILL'S TOP FAMILY ADVENTURES IN WEST MICHIGAN–SOUTH

1. Warren Dunes State Park, Bridgman
2. Kalamazoo Aviation History Museum, Kalamazoo
3. Echo Valley Tobogganing, Kalamazoo
4. Perch Fishing, South Haven
5. Grand Rapids museums, Grand Rapids

Greek Revival, Gothic Revival, and Queen Anne style. If you can't make it for the show, self-guiding maps are available from local shops and inns and at **Honolulu House,** an 1860 Victorian home with a Hawaiian bent added by its previous owner, a former U.S. consul to Hawaii. Another Marshall landmark is **Schuler's Restaurant,** where a variety of entrees is topped by its famed prime rib, served in an 1870 inn. For home tour and other information, contact the chamber of commerce at (800) 877–5163. Honolulu House is open daily from noon to 5:00 P.M. between May and October. Admission is $3.00 for adults, $2.00 for anyone twelve to eighteen, and $2.50 for seniors; kids under twelve are free. Tickets to the home tour are $10.00 before August 31, $12.00 afterward. Schuler's is at 115 South Eagle Street; for reservation information call (616) 781–0600.

BATTLE CREEK

While the city that cereal built no longer features tours of the Kellogg Company, Ralston Purina, and Post—protecting trade secrets was the reason, the companies said—the city throws a party the second Saturday in June during its **Cereal Fest,** starting with the World's Longest Breakfast Table. How long? How about 250 picnic tables end to end, groaning under boxes of cereal, milk, juice, donuts, and Kellogg's Pop Tarts. The free feast, which runs from 8:00 A.M. to noon along Michigan Avenue downtown, feeds some 60,000 celebrants each year. On the Friday night before, a grand parade, including a costumed children's contingent, wends through the downtown area. Saturday, children's activities ranging from face painting to rescue demonstrations and other entertainment fill up the time through midnight.

Each July, Battle Creek residents turn their eyes to the skies as the **Hot Air Balloon Championship and Air Show** fills eight days starting the Saturday before the Fourth of July holiday. The competition draws up to 200 balloon fliers to the city for takeoffs weather permitting, from W. K. Kellogg Airport. During the air show, see the likes of the Air Force's Thunderbirds or the U.S. Navy's Blue Angels perform precision maneuvers. Your kids will love the wing walkers and stunt planes, not to mention their chance to inspect aircraft up close during on-the-ground displays. Entry to the site requires a parking fee of $4.00 per day for cars or $10.00 for RVs. The airport is reached by exiting Interstate 94 at Helmer Road and following the signs. For balloon show information call (616) 962–0592. For Cereal Fest details call (800) 397–2240 or (616) 962–2240.

Come winter, the city literally glows as its streets are lit by more than one million festive lights—most of them centered around the renovated Kalamazoo River commercial area—during the city's **Festival of Lights,** held annually from mid-November through December 31. The city's **Linear Park** traverses much of the city, offering 17 miles of walkways, gazebos, boardwalks, and bridges along the river. To reach the festival area, take exit 98B off Interstate 94 and go north into downtown. Other events taking place in conjunction with the lights festival include animal-themed displays of illumination at **Binder Park Zoo.** The zoo itself contains more than eighty animal exhibits and is open normally from April 13 through October 13. There's also a hands-on playground at **Miller Children's Zoo,** part of Binder Park. The zoo is 3 miles south of Interstate 94 exit 100, at 7400 Division Drive. Hours are 9:00 A.M. to 5:00 P.M. weekdays (and till 8:00 P.M. on Wednesday only in summer), 9:00 A.M. to 6:00 P.M. Saturday, and 11:00 A.M. to 6:00 P.M. Sunday. Admission is $4.75 for adults and teens, $2.75 for children three through twelve, and $3.75 for seniors.

Inside the seventy-two-acre **Leila Arboretum** is the **Kingman Museum of Natural History,** which features three floors of exhibits. You can delve into the age of dinosaurs if you like, or explore the universe in the planetarium. The arboretum and the museum are at West Michigan Avenue and Twentieth Street. To get there take exit 95 off Interstate 94 and travel north on Helmer for about 6 miles to West Michigan Avenue; from there, head east 1½ miles, then north into the arboretum. Museum hours are 9:00 A.M. to 5:00 P.M. Monday through Friday and 1:00 to 5:00 P.M. on Saturday. Admission is $2.00 for adults and $1.00 for students. Call (616) 965–5117 to find out more about the museum, or (616) 969–0270 for information about the arboretum, which is open daily dawn to dusk and is free.

Outside the city, on Wintergreen Lake, about 13 miles to the northwest, is the **Kellogg Bird Sanctuary,** part of Michigan State University. Ducks, geese, pheasant, swans, and other feathered life can be seen along a 1-mile nature trail and from an observation deck over the lake. To get to the sanctuary, take exit 80 (Sprinkle Road) off Interstate 94, head north to Gull Road (Michigan 43), and turn east. Go through Richland—Michigan 43 becomes Michigan 89—and proceed 4½ miles east. Turn north onto Fortieth Street and then west onto C Avenue and watch for the signs to Waterford Drive. The sanctuary is open from 9:00 A.M. to 8:00 P.M. between May and October, and from 9:00 A.M. to 5:00 P.M. the rest of the year. Admission is $2.00 for adults and teens and 50 cents for children ages four through twelve. Phone (616) 671–2510 for more information.

Like baseball? The **Battle Creek Battlecats** took to the field for the first time in 1995. A Class A farm team for the Boston Red Sox, the team plays in the 6,200-seat **C. O. Brown Stadium,** home of the annual Stan Musial World Series for high-schoolers and the NCAA Championships. Ticket prices are $5.00 for box seats, $4.00 for reserved, and $3.00 for bleachers. Senior citizens pay $2.00. Many nights feature special promotions, such as free hats or balls or fireworks. The team plays seventy games at home. Call (616) 660–BALL for ticket information and reservations. The stadium is at 1392 Capitol Avenue. Reach it by taking exit 98B off Interstate 94 and going north. The road becomes Capitol Avenue, which will take you through town to Bailey Park and the field. For general Battle Creek information, call the Greater Battle Creek/Calhoun County Visitors Bureau, at (616) 962–2240.

HICKORY CORNERS

At the **Gilmore Classic Car Museum,** you'll find more than 120 preserved beauties that epitomize the term *rolling sculpture.* They're all on display in an antique barn in the tiny town of Hickory Corners, just northwest of Battle Creek. The collection includes a rare 1899 Locomobile Steamer and a 1910 Rolls-Royce Silver Ghost. Along with the autos and a replica of the Wright brothers plane, there's a narrow-gauge locomotive, plus picnic and playground areas where the kids can blow off steam. Museum hours are 10:00 A.M. to 5:00 P.M. daily from May 1 through October 29. Admission is $5.00 for adults, $4.00 for seniors, $2.00 for children ages seven through fifteen (kids six and under get in free). The museum is at 6865 Hickory Road. Take Michigan 43 north from Kalamazoo to Hickory. For more information, call (616) 671–5089.

KALAMAZOO

From maple sugaring in season to a walk-by history of aviation at its "Air Zoo," this city along Interstate 94 delivers a memorable visit for the entire family. At the

Kalamazoo Nature Center north of the city, 1,000 acres of dense hardwood forest awaits exploration. It's all detailed at the visitors center. A pioneer homestead with depictions of early Michigan farm life operates during warm weather. The nature center is at 7000 North Westnedge. Go north from Interstate 94 at U.S. 131 and get off at exit 44 (D Avenue); drive east to Westnedge, then south less than a mile. The visitors center is open from 9:00 A.M. to 5:00 P.M. Monday through Saturday and from 1:00 to 5:00 P.M. Sunday. The grounds are open one hour later. Admission is $3.00 for adults and $1.50 for children four through seventeen. For more information call (616) 381–1574.

South of the city, the **Kalamazoo Aviation History Museum** is one of the state's best. At times more than fifty aircraft are on display in a large hangar, an adjacent annex, and outside. Let the kids climb in and "fly" a flight simulator. At 2:00 and 7:00 P.M. on Wednesdays from May through October, you can ride in an antique Ford Tri-Motor for $35 per person. You'll also see military uniforms, and model aircraft, and there's a gift shop, too. Take Interstate 94 exit 78 south onto Portage Road and go about 1½ miles to Milham Road; then head east ½ mile to 3101 East Milham. Nonsummer hours are 9:00 A.M. to 5:00 P.M. Monday through Saturday and noon to 5:00 P.M. on Sunday; from June through August the museum stays open an hour later. Admission is $5.00 for adults, $4.00 for seniors, $3.00 for children six through fifteen, and $1.00 for three- to five-year-olds. For more information call (616) 382–6555. The annual **High on Kalamazoo air show** takes place the second weekend in June at the airport. Call (616) 381–8237 for details.

The family fun in Kalamazoo doesn't stop for winter. Remember those butterflies in your stomach at just the moment your sled or toboggan moved down your neighborhood winter hill? You and your kids can experience the same roller-coaster thrill at **Echo Valley,** east of the city. Eight iced tracks await. For $6.00 per adult (all-day pass $10.00), you'll get use of a wooden toboggan. Load it onto one of the tracks and you'll be launched down a 120-foot hill at up to 60 miles per hour, over a quarter-mile of curves and straights. A rope tow gets you back to the top. Cold noses and toes can be warmed at the lodge while you sample the offerings at the snack bar. Then strap on a pair of rental skates ($2.50 for skating, rentals are $1.50) and try the 43,000-square-foot outdoor rink. To reach Echo Valley, exit Interstate 94 at Sprinkle Road, take it north to Eighth Avenue, and turn east; the entrance is 3 miles away. For conditions and times of operation, call (616) 349–3291. For more on the area, call the Kalamazoo County Convention and Visitors Bureau at (616) 381–4003.

MATTAWAN

Know how big the largest salmon ever caught in the state is? Or what fish lives in Michigan but reproduces thousands of miles away in the ocean? And what "Great Lakes invaders" are? Learn those answers and more at the **Michigan Fisheries Interpretive Center,** on the grounds of the **Wolf Lake State Fish Hatchery,** west of Kalamazoo in Mattawan. See engravings of forty-six "state record" fish, plus an authentic Au Sable riverboat hanging above the reception desk. Dioramas explain each type of Michigan lake and stream, from warm to cold water. Then go outside to the fish ponds and feed the inhabitants, which are up to 5 feet long. (The answer to that fishy question about which species reproduces in the ocean? The American eel, which migrates to Bermuda to spawn.) From U.S. 131, take exit 38B, north of Interstate 94; the center is 6 miles west on Michigan 43. Hours are 10:00 A.M. to 5:00 P.M. Wednesday through Saturday and noon to 5:00 P.M. on Sunday. Admission is free. For more information call (616) 668–2876.

PAW PAW

Paw Paw has been the center of Michigan's primary wine-making industry since the early 1900s (not counting Prohibition). While other sites, including the Traverse City area, have also developed, it remains one of the best areas to sample state vintages.

Learn all you ever wanted to know about the fishes of Michigan and beyond at the Michigan Fisheries Interpretive Center.

Two wineries, **St. Julian,** Michigan's oldest, and **Warner,** the state's largest, offer tours of the harvesting, pressing, and cellaring. Tasting rooms offer samples and a chance to buy some wine to take home. Tours are free. To reach both wineries, take exit 60 off Interstate 94 and head north. St. Julian (open 9:00 A.M. to 5:00 P.M. Monday through Saturday and noon to 5:00 P.M. on Sunday) is at 716 South Kalamazoo; call (616) 657–5568. Warner (open from 9:00 A.M. to 6:00 P.M. Monday through Saturday and from noon to 6:00 P.M. on Sunday) is at 706 South Kalamazoo Street; call (616) 657–3165.

In early September the town hosts the yearly **Wine and Harvest Festival,** which features an annual parade and the grape stomp—the team of five producing the most juice wins—plus numerous other events. For information call the Paw Paw Chamber of Commerce at (616) 657–5395.

Other wineries in the vicinity include **Fenn Valley** (616–561–2396), **Peterson and Sons** (in Kalamazoo 616–626–9755), **Baroda's Heart of the Vineyard** (616–422–1617), **New Era's Tartan Hill** (616–861–4657), **Lemon Creek Winery** (616–471–1321), and **Le Monteux Vineyards** (in the Grand Rapids area, 616–784–4554).

BENTON HARBOR/ST. JOSEPH

These twin cities on the Lake Michigan shore mark the heart of Michigan's harbor country, where state residents and those from neighboring areas come to relax. Head to Benton Harbor and St. Joseph the first week of May for the annual **Blossomtime Festival,** which is highlighted by the Blessing of the Blossoms in the fruit and berry orchards surrounding the city, arts-and-crafts sales, and the Grand Floral Parade. Later on in the summer, you can stop along Old U.S. 31 (also sometimes called A-2) and **pick your own blueberries** and other delectables at any of several farms in the region. The cities are reached just off Interstate 94. For festival information call (616) 926–7397. **Salmon, steelhead, and other fishing charters** also are available along the St. Joseph River, which separates the two cities.

In downtown St. Joseph, the **Curious Kids Museum** is a great hands-on learning experience for children that revolves around the area's orchard crops. Kids can pick apples from simulated trees and try on a different costume at each exhibit. The museum is at 415 Lake Boulevard. Hours are 10:00 A.M. to 5:00 P.M. Wednesday through Saturday and noon to 5:00 P.M. on Sunday. In summer the museum is also open from 10:00 A.M. to 5:00 P.M. on Monday and Tuesday. Admission is $3.00 for adults and $2.50 for anyone two to eighteen years old. Reach the museum by taking exit 27 off Interstate 94 and heading north on Niles Avenue; turn west on Broad, go 2 blocks, and then proceed south on Lake Boulevard. For more details call (616) 983–2543. For other information on activities around this region and in both cities, call (616) 925–6301 or (616) 925–6100.

SOUTH HAVEN

Just up the road a few miles is a lakeside town that will remind you a lot of New England. South Haven's businesses abut the Black River, which flows right through town. If you've got a fishing license, don't miss the next departure of the perch party boats run by **Captain Nichols** (616–637–2507) or **Captain Chuck's** (616–637–8007). They both take up to forty anglers per trip on daily fishing outings that leave the dock at 8:00 A.M. Adults pay $25 to $30 each, and the crews will even clean your catch. To reserve a spot stop at the booths downtown. Afterward, browse the quaint streets, or in summer head for the great Lake Michigan city beach.

Across the river from the perch boats, the **Lake Michigan Maritime Museum** will introduce your family to the role of the Great Lakes and boating in Michigan's development. Exhibits start with watercraft made by Native Americans and proceed through present-day commercial craft. There's a large exhibit on the Chris Craft Company—boat manufacturer that had three plants in Michigan—and one on the U.S. Lifesaving Service, precursor of the U.S. Coast Guard. The museum, perch boats, and other attractions are off Interstate 196 at exit 20; take Phoenix Road west toward the lake. The museum is on Dyckman Avenue and the Black River bridge. Hours from May through October are 10:00 A.M. to 5:00 P.M. daily. Guided tours are available through August. Call (616) 637–8078 for information about hours the rest of the year. South Haven's annual **Harborfest** is in mid-June and **Van Buren State Park** with camping along the beach is nearby. For more on the area, call (616) 637–5252 or (800) SO–HAVEN.

SAUGATUCK/DOUGLAS

The **Saugaduck Festival** is not the largest pageant in the state, but the annual event promises plenty of good fun in this artists' colony tucked in the high dunes along Lake Michigan. A takeoff on the nearby Fennville Goose Festival, which celebrates the return of some 300,000 Canada (please, don't say "Canadian") geese annually, this one celebrates the return of about 2,200 mallard ducks to the waterfront of Gleason's Party Store and Marina each spring. On the first Saturday after Father's Day, an annual parade features the precision movements of the Saugatuck/Douglas Lawn Mower and Mulching Drill Team, among other laughable entries. There's also storytelling for children narrated by Mother Goose and a web-footed waddle race for the kids. What better place to have an arts-and-crafts show? Don't forget to visit the area's galleries for locally produced art, and while you're there be sure to ride the **hand-operated chain ferry** over the Kalamazoo River. You can also try your hand at salmon fishing on a charter boat or take a ninety-minute cruise on the Kalamazoo River and Lake Michigan aboard the *Star of Saugatuck* ($7.60 for adults and teens, $4.00 for kids three through twelve). Saugatuck is west of Interstate 196 at exit 41 (Blue Star Highway). For information on the festival and other events, call (616) 857–1701. The chain ferry is for pedestrians and bicyclists and operates mid-June through Labor Day. Fare one way is $1.00 for adults, 50 cents for children. For schedule information call (616) 857–2603. For more on the *Star of Saugatuck,* which operates from mid-May to late October, call (616) 857–4261.

Just across the mouth of the Kalamazoo is Douglas, home to the *SS Keewatin,* a museum of lore from when steam ruled the Great Lakes and liners like the 350-foot-long *Keewatin* were commonplace. The ship was the last of the classic steamships. It sailed the lakes for fifty-seven summers and now is part of **Harbor Village.** Tours of the ship take visitors inside its elegant captain's quarters to learn about the age of steam travel on the lakes. Admission is $4.00 for teens and adults and $2.00 for children twelve and under. The site also includes the *City of Douglas,* a sightseeing cruiser that offers lunch and dinner trips, and is the home of the *Calypso,* which cruises on Lake Michigan daily, complete with Caribbean music ($6.00 for teens and adults, $4.00 for children twelve and under). From Memorial Day through Labor Day the City of Douglas leaves daily for lunch (about $16.50, fare included), afternoon sightseeing ($9.00), and dinner cruises ($32.00), and also features Sunday brunch ($28.00, children $3.00 off). All three vessels are located along Highway A-2, near the Saugatuck-Douglas bridge. Call (616) 857–2464 or (616) 857–2107 for more information.

Saugatuck visitors can also take sightseeing trips over the nearby dunes from May through mid-October. Take exit 41 (Saugatuck) from Interstate 196 and go south on Blue Star Highway about a half mile. Price is $9.50 for teens and adults, $6.00 for kids three through ten. Rides start at 10:00 A.M. Monday through Saturday and at noon on Sunday; the last ride leaves at 5:30 P.M. Call (616) 857–2253 for more details.

HOLLAND

A visit to this quaint city gives you a taste of the area's Dutch history. On a visit to **Windmill Island,** cross an authentic Dutch drawbridge to see the 200-year-old De Zwann windmill, which still operates, producing flour sold at the park. There's also a miniature Dutch village where there are dancing demonstrations and guided tours in summer. The thirty-acre island is downtown at Seventh Street and Lincoln Avenue and is open from May through October. Admission is $5.00 for teens and adults and $2.50 for children ages five through twelve. Hours vary through the summer; call (616) 355–1030.

The city was also a famous furniture-making center—like its neighbor, Grand Rapids, 30 miles to the east——and the **Baker Furniture Museum** has antiques and copies dating from the 1500s. The museum is at 100 East Eighth, between College and Columbia avenues. The museum is open April through October, from 10:00 A.M. to 5:00 P.M. Monday through Friday and from 9:00 A.M. to noon on Saturday. Admission costs $2.00 for anyone twelve or older; call (616) 392–8761 or 392–3181. The **Holland Museum** also features exhibits on local history. It's at 31 West Tenth Street downtown and is open Monday, Wednesday, Friday, and Saturday from 10:00 A.M. to 5:00 P.M., Thursday from 10:00 A.M. to 8:00 P.M., and Sunday from 2:00 to 5:00 P.M. Admission is $3.00 for adults, $2.00 for seniors and children six through twelve, and free for kids five and under; call (616) 392–9084.

Also worth a stop is the **De Klomp Wooden Shoe and Delftware Factory.** As many as 90 percent of the locals you'll see are of Dutch descent, left from when the area was settled in 1846 by religious-freedom seekers. The immigrants brought their crafts with them, and two examples can be seen here. Artisans continue to create the blue-and-white delftware ceramics produced at De Klomp, the only delft factory in the nation, while in another area skilled experts gouge, carve, and shape blocks of wood into shoes.

Next door, at the **Veldheer Tulip Gardens,** more than a hundred varieties of tulips bloom each spring along U.S. 31, and visitors who stop can purchase bulbs. The factory and the gardens are 3 miles north of the city. Combined admission is $2.50 for adults and $1.00 for children ages five through sixteen. Call (616) 399–1900 for hours, which vary throughout the year.

The city of Holland is a major producer of bulbs and its heritage is celebrated each May during the **Tulip Time Festival,** one of Michigan's first warm-weather outdoor events, which features 8 miles of blooming tulips planted along city streets. Local shopping includes a large discount mall. For more call the convention bureau at (616) 396–4221.

GRAND RAPIDS

While the rapids that named this city are long covered under dams, you can see one of the state's minor-league baseball teams in action, explore a museum portraying the city's past, stroll through sculpture gardens, and perhaps even wet a fishing line downtown.

The **Van Andel Museum Center and Public Museum of Grand Rapids** is located on the west bank of the Grand River, which flows through town. The $40-million complex traces the city from its start as a trading post to its peak as an industrial center known worldwide for furniture production. While most of the manufacturing has gone to the South, the museum shows the city's heyday through artifacts, photos, and videos. Antique buffs will like the more than 120 types of finished furniture displayed, featuring several periods. Other exhibits include a re-creation of downtown at the turn of the century and one on West Michigan's first inhabitants, Native Americans. For kids and the young at heart, there's a 1928 carousel in a pavilion over the river, accompanied by an old Wurlitzer organ.

A short walk to the north, see the **Gerald R. Ford Museum,** dedicated to the hometown boy made good, who was president following Richard Nixon's resignation. Displays detail Ford's private and public lives, and include an exact replica of the Ford Oval Office.

Just up the river, join in the fun fishing for salmon in fall or steelhead in spring at the **Fish Ladder Sculpture** at Leonard and Front streets. The structure helps fish climb a 6-foot-high dam. Best times to see them are in September and October.

Take in some greenery at the **Michigan Botanic Garden and Meijer Sculpture Park,** commonly known as **Frederik Meijer Gardens,** a seventy-acre sanctuary of tropical and other plants from five continents. At five stories tall, the indoor conservatory is Michigan's largest. Mixed in with coconut palms from the Pacific, ficus from India, and orchids from South America are dozens of sculptures by American artists, such as Michigan's Marshall Fredericks. There's a restaurant inside, too, plus free tours and docents to answer questions.

The city's **Old Kent Park** isn't old at all. Completed in 1994, it's home to the **Grand Rapids Whitecaps,** a Class A farm team for the Oakland Athletics. Up to 10,000 can watch seventy home games a year. Take your lawn chair and wait with the kids for that foul ball in a special grassy area set aside for folks who want to watch the game the way spectators did when it was invented. Ticket prices are $6.00 for box seats, $4.50 for reserved, and $3.00 for the lawn.

John Ball Park Zoo is one of the state's largest, with 500 animals from across the world plus a new attraction, the **Living Shores Aquarium.** The **Blandford Nature Center** presents nature programs and offers self-guided trails. Depending on the weather, there are maple-syrup-making demonstrations each March; call ahead.

ANNUAL EVENTS FOR THE FAMILY IN WEST MICHIGAN—SOUTH

Tuliptime Festival, mid-May, Holland, (616) 396–4221

High on Kalamazoo Air Show, mid-June, Kalamazoo Airport, (616) 381–8237

Cereal Fest, second Saturday in June, Battle Creek, (800) 397–2240

International Cherry Pit Spit, first Saturday in July, Tree-Mendus Fruit Farm, (616) 782–962–7101

Battle Creek Hot Air Balloon Championships, Saturday before July 4, Kellogg Airport, (615) 962–0592

South Haven Annual Blueberry Festival, mid-August, South Haven, (616) 637–5171

Michigan Wine and Harvest Festival, summer, Paw Paw, (616) 657–5395

To top off your stay in Grand Rapids, **AJ's Family Water Park** has five water rides, a wave pool, minigolf, a kiddie pool, and more.

The Public Museum (616–456–3966) is at 272 Pearl Street. Hours are 9:00 A.M. to 5:00 P.M. daily. Admission is $5.00 for adults, $4.00 for seniors, $2.00 for children and teens from three through seventeen. The Ford Museum (616–451–9263), at 303 Pearl, operates from 9:00 A.M. to 4:45 P.M. Monday through Saturday and from noon to 4:45 on Sunday. Admission is $2.00 for adults, $1.50 for seniors, and free for anyone under fifteen. To get there exit U.S. 131 at 85B (Pearl Street) and go east.

Meijer Gardens is at 3411 Bradford NE. From Interstate 96 take the East Beltline exit and go north 1 block to Bradford; then turn east and drive about half a mile. The gardens are open daily from 9:00 A.M. to 6:00 P.M. except Wednesday, when the park stays open until 8 P.M. Admission is $3.50 for adults, $3.00 for seniors, and $1.50 for anyone five through thirteen. For information call (616) 957–1580.

The Whitecaps' Old Kent Park is at U.S. 131 and West River Drive. The exit is about 5 miles north of downtown. For game times call (616) 784–4131.

John Ball Zoo is at Interstate 196 and Michigan 45, 2 miles west from down-town on Fulton. It's open daily from 10:00 A.M. to 6:00 P.M. mid-May to Labor Day and from 10:00 A.M. to 4:00 P.M. the rest of the year. Admission is $3.00 for persons fourteen through sixty-two, $1.50 for seniors, and $2.00 for kids five through thirteen. Children four and under are let in for free—and so is everybody else from December through February, when the entrance fee is waived. Phone (616) 336–4300 or (616) 336–4301 for information.

Blandford Nature Center (616–453–6192) is at 1715 Hillburn NW. Take the Leonard Street exit off U.S. 131 and drive west 4 miles, turn north onto Hillburn, and follow the signs. Hours are 9:00 A.M. to 5:00 P.M. Monday through Friday, and 1:00 to 5:00 P.M. on weekends.

AJ's Water Park, 4441 Twenty-eighth Street, SE, is reached by taking exit 43A (Twenty-eighth Street West) and driving 1 mile. It's open 11:00 A.M. to 8:00 P.M. from Memorial Day weekend through August 28 and from 11:00 A.M. to 6:00 P.M. from September 1 through September 4. Admission is $12.95—$9.95 for anyone under forty-eight inches tall—with discounts offered after 4:00 P.M.; everyone over fifty-nine and under four gets in free. Call (616) 940–0400 for details.

For more on what to see and do around the city, call the Grand Rapids/Kent County Convention and Visitors Bureau at (616) 459–8287 or (800) 678–9859.

ADA

See the company that SA-8 built. Started as a small garage business by two friends who thought up a different way to sell laundry soap, the **Amway Corporation** grew from their idea to become the largest company in the world using home-based operations to distribute its products. Take a free, one-hour guided tour (at 9:00 and 11:00 A.M. and 1:00 and 3:00 P.M., Monday through Friday) to see the company's research-and-development and printing opera-tions. Amway is at 7575 Fulton Street E, 5 miles east of Interstate 96 at Michigan 21. Call (616) 787–6701 for information.

HASTINGS

Southeastern Michigan has Greenfield Village and the Henry Ford Museum. Flint has Crossroads Village. But the town of Hastings, population only 6,500, has a historic village on a par with the big boys in its **Charlton Park Village and Museum.** Sixteen buildings help re-create an 1890s Michigan town; in addition, you'll find a beach, a playground, and a boat launch, on more than

300 acres. In the village there's everything from a blacksmith's to a school-house. Christmas is one of the most decorative times, as buildings are lit by candlelight, starting on the first two weekends in December from noon to 5:00 P.M. Charlton Park is at 2545 South Charlton Park Road, a quarter-mile north of M-79 between Hastings and Nashville. Travel north from Interstate 94 on Michigan 66, then turn west on Michigan 79, then heading 2 miles south and 4 miles east on Michigan 79. From Memorial Day to mid-September, hours are 9:00 A.M. to 5:00 P.M. Admission is $3.00 for adults, $2.00 for persons over fifty-five, and $1.00 for anyone five through fifteen. Special events cost $4.00 for adults, and $1.00 for children; call (616) 945–3775 for detailed information.

CEDAR SPRINGS

Lumberjacks wore 'em. So did some of the greatest comedy stars. And you, too, can own a pair of the original trapdoor red flannels that have been made at Cedar Springs for the past fifty-eight years. It all started when a *New York Times* editorial fussed that red flannels were hard to find in winter. The local paper shot back that the town had plenty. To meet demand a factory produced the union suits and other items, but now that job has been taken over by local residents, who supply exclusively the **Cedar Sweets and Specialty Shop** at 37 South Main Street downtown. Other items for sale at the store include nightshirts and boxer sets, popular with the college and high-school crowd, plus old-fashioned nightshirts and more. Prices for the original drop-drawer long johns range from $32.95 to $17.95 for infant sizes. Store hours are 9:00 A.M. to 5:00 P.M. Tuesday through Thursday, 9:00 A.M. to 6:00 P.M. Friday, and 11:00 A.M. to 3:00 P.M. Saturday. For information call (616) 696–3821.

On the last weekend of September and first weekend of October, the town's **Red Flannel Festival** pays its respect to the clothing that put Cedar Springs on the map. There are two parades on the first weekend of October, arts-and-crafts vendors, and even the crowning of a red-flannel queen. The local historical museum (616–696–2584) also features an entire section on the history of red flannels. There is no admission fee for the festival except for individual events and special attractions. The museum is in Morley Park; summer hours are 1:30 to 4:00 P.M. Sunday and admission is free. Cedar Springs is at exit 104 off U.S. 131, 15 miles north of Grand Rapids; head east 2 miles to downtown. For festival information call (616) 696–2662.

GRAND HAVEN

Families start gathering just before sundown, and by nightfall the grandstand, which holds 2,500, is usually filled. The harbor, where the Grand River ends its journey across Lower Michigan at Lake Michigan, is dotted with boat lights as, suddenly, a dune erupts in color, water plumes, and music. They've come as they have in summer for more than thirty years for another performance of the **Musical Fountain,** which bursts to life nightly about 9:45 P.M. from Memorial Day through Labor Day and on September weekends. The fountain spews jets of water up to 125 feet in the air—and best of all, the show's free.

During the day trolleys take visitors up and down the beachfront, and the annual **Coast Guard Festival** features a parade, fireworks, and ship tours the last week of July and first week of August. Hop aboard the *Harbor Steamer* for a ninety-minute cruise-tour of Spring Lake. Grand Haven is reached by taking the city exit off Interstate 96. For information call (800) 303–4096 or (616) 842–4499.

If you come here in mid-May and someone in town tells you to go fly a kite, he or she just might be directing you to the golden sand beach, with blue Lake Michigan as the background, where you'll join up to 40,000 spectators to watch kites up to half a football field long fill the air during the annual **Great Lakes Sport Kite Championships.**

Bob Negen—who began his Mackinac Kite Company on a whim, after seeing his dad pick up a kite and go sky high over it in the early 1980s—annually hosts the event from his store in town. What'll you see? According to Negen, some of the world's finest stunt and sport kite pilots.

These kites are a bit different than the ones you buy at the local hardware for your kids—the kind that eventually wind up in your front-yard tree. Sport kites are controlled by two lines that pilots use to steer. Flying them individually and in teams, competitors must duplicate three predetermined maneuvers and initiate moves of their own invention during two- to four-minute routines. Five judges then score for execution and style. In ballet events flyers must choreograph their flights to music and are judged mostly on artistic interpretation, plus how well they execute difficult maneuvers. Events run Friday through Sunday and include a Friday-night fly at which lights attached to the kites and lines create a spectacular show. Relive your childhood and try your own hand during free stunt kite lessons for beginners. You can't beat the location: the sugar sand beach of **Grand Haven State Park.**

If you get hooked by the competition, stop by Negen's store at 116 Washington. You can pick from more than a hundreds types of kites, from indoor models that take only a whiff of air to fly to the newest trend, power kites, with up to fifty-five square feet of surface. You can even try your hand at a 150-foot-long dragon kite with a mouth 15 feet in diameter. (If you can't make it to Grand Haven, stop by Negen's other store, in Mackinaw City, during Father's Day weekend for the annual **Mackinaw City Kite Festival.** Family fun runs from free kites for the kids to demonstrations of Japanese fighting kites battling to cut opponents out of the sky.) Viewing the championships is free with admission to Grand Haven State Park. Grand Haven is reached by taking exit 9 (Michigan 104) off Interstate 96 and heading west. Call the Negen's Grand Haven store at (616) 846–7501. Grand Haven State Park, which has camping on the beach, can be reached at (616) 798–3711.

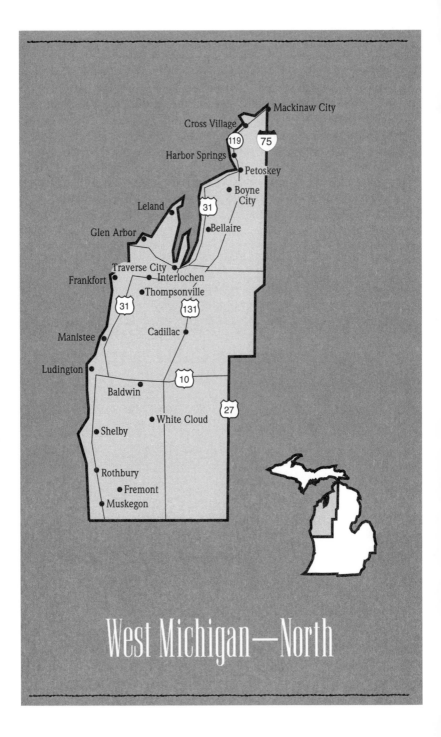

Mackinaw City

Cross Village

119 75

Harbor Springs

Petoskey

Boyne
City

Leland

31

Glen Arbor

Bellaire

Traverse City
Interlochen

Frankfort

Thompsonville

31

131

Manistee

Cadillac

Ludington

10

Baldwin

27

White Cloud

Shelby

Rothbury

Fremont

Muskegon

West Michigan—North

West Michigan—North

The northern part of West Michigan takes in some of the state's most inviting places to visit, from former industrial towns on the verge of finding new life as tourist destinations, to small towns that are growing by leaps and bounds, to others that nearly close in winter.

MUSKEGON

Welcome to Muskegon, the Lumber Queen City. In the last century Muskegon's now-razed mills and surrounding forests of white pine provided the lumber to rebuild Chicago after its fire and to construct homes in much of the West.

Top billing in summer goes to the **Air Fair** at Muskegon County Airport in mid-July. Some of the largest, smallest, and fastest aircraft in the world participate in the three-day show, which also has up to 120 aircraft on display along the flight line, where some pilots will let young children climb in and sit at the controls.

For beachgoers, Muskegon County has nine public expanses along 26 miles of shore, including the beaches at **Pere Marquette Park** in the city and at **Muskegon State Park** to the north. Across the Muskegon River outlet, board the *USS Silversides*, billed as the country's most famous surviving World War II submarine; or head south to **P. J. Hoffmaster State Park** and its **E. Genevieve Gillette Visitors Center,** where kids can learn how the shore sand dunes were formed.

Other summer fun awaits you at **Michigan's Adventure Amusement Park,** the state's largest. Stare down from the 90-foot crest of the first hill on the "Wolverine Wildcat," a wooden roller coaster, or try the tamer rides. If getting wet sounds like fun, visit **Wild Water Adventure** or its competition, **Pleasure Island.**

History buffs will appreciate the **Hackley and Hume houses,** built by lumber baron partners next door to each other near downtown. The Hackley residence is judged to be the finest Gilded Age home in America.

In cold weather, hold your own family Winter Olympics and ride a luge at the **Muskegon Winter Sports Complex.** Here's a place for the kids to live up to their "No Fear" hats and slip down an ice-covered, banked track on a sled barely a yard long, faster than Dad or Mom.

Michigan's Adventure is 8 miles north of Muskegon on U.S. 31 at Russell Road and is open daily from Memorial Day through Labor Day. Admission is $15 for adults; children two and under are free. Phone (616) 766–3377 for information. Pleasure Island is 6 miles south of the city on U.S. 31 and 1½ miles west on Pontaluna Road. It's open Memorial Day weekend through Labor Day. Admission is $15.95 for adults, $7.95 for seniors, and $9.95 for children four and under; phone (616) 798–7857 for hours.

The *Silversides* is at 1346 Bluff at Pere Marquette Park and is open from April through October. Admission is $3.50 for adults, $1.50 for children five through eleven, and $2.00 for anyone sixty-two or older; kids four and under are free. For specific hours call (616) 755–1230. To reach Hoffmaster State Park, exit U.S. 31 at Pontaluna Road and drive west 2 miles; call (616) 798–3711 for information. To reach Muskegon State Park, take Michigan 120 (the Fremont exit) west off U.S. 31 and follow the signs west onto Lake Avenue; then go west on Ruddiman, which becomes Memorial Drive. The park is about 5 miles down the road, and the sports complex is at the park. Call (616) 744–9629 for track conditions. For area information, call (616) 772–3551.

ROTHBURY

Hold on, pardner. You mean there's a real dude ranch in Michigan? Yup. In fact, the **Double JJ** is one of three in the state. Hit the trail here on daily rides headed by the staff of western wranglers, who'll teach you the intricacies of "trottin' and lopin'" (trotting and cantering, for you city slickers).

A highlight of the week is the rodeo, where new cowboys can test their skills. Previously, Double JJ was for grown-ups only, but new in 1996 is a camp where parents drop their cowkids off and forget about them for the day—the **Back 40 Kids Resort.** Each generation has fun independently and learns ranch skills without the other. Parents and kids can meet up at the end of each

BILL'S TOP FAMILY ADVENTURES IN WEST MICHIGAN–NORTH

1. Michigan's Adventure Amusement Park, Muskegon
2. Mac Woods' Dune Rides, Silver Lake Dunes
3. SS Badger, Ludington
4. Sleeping Bear Dunes National Lakeshore, Glen Arbor
5. Mackinaw City

day, if they wish. There's nightly music in the dance hall for the adults (kids will have entertainment, too), fishing in a private lake, and even **The Thoroughbred,** an eighteen-hole Arthur Hills–designed championship golf course rated one of the nation's best. Parents can stay in original cabins or new condos near the golf course. To get to Double JJ, take the Rothbury exit (exit 136, Winston Road) off U.S. 31 and go east about a quarter-mile; then travel north on Water Road about 1 mile and watch for the signs. A week's stay starts at $549 per person, including meals. For details and reservations call (616) 894–4444.

FREMONT

Most of us leave it to the babies to gum down on the millions of containers of strained peaches, apricots, and meat that rolls out the door at the **Gerber Products Company,** founded in 1928. Now it's your family's turn. During the **National Baby Food Festival,** held annually here the third weekend in July, don your bib and dig in during the baby food–eating contest! You might even win some cash if you can down five jars of the stuff before your neighbor. Other events in the weeklong fest include a car show, a midway, and a downtown parade. The company began when Mrs. Gerber told Mr. G. she was tired of making her own baby food and couldn't he try making some at his canning plant. The rest is pabulum history. Fremont is about an hour north of Grand Rapids and is reached off U.S. 131 by turning west at Michigan 82 and following it into the city. For festival information call (616) 924–2270.

WHITEHALL/MONTAGUE

The **White River Light Station Museum,** in an 1875 lighthouse on the Lake Michigan beach along the mouth of the White River, is a repository for photos and artifacts that tell the story of those who worked here and risked their lives to save others in trouble, plus a collection of memorabilia recalling the vacation steamers that ran between here and Chicago. From Memorial Day weekend through Labor Day, it's open 11:00 A.M. to 5:00 p.m. Tuesday through Friday and noon to 6:00 p.m. on weekends, and in May and September it's open weekends only from noon to 6:00 p.m. Admission is $2.00 for adults, $1.00 for persons ten through eighteen, and free for children age nine or under. It's at 6199 Murray Road. Drive west of the city off U.S. 31 on White Lake Drive and take South Shore Drive west to Murray Road. Call (616) 894-8265.

While you're there, don't forget to take the kids to see what's billed as the **world's largest weather vane,** on the Montague side of the Montague–Whitehall bridge. It's on display at the Whitehall Products factory showroom in the **Corner House of Gifts** in Whitehall, where you pick out a vane to take home. Prices start at $38. The shop is located at 225 East Colby, at the Colby Road exit off U.S. 31. It's open from 10:00 A.M. to 5:30 p.m. Monday through Saturday, and from noon to 4:00 p.m. Sunday in July, August, and November. Call (616) 893-5235 for information.

WHITE CLOUD

If you don't come here to see the Muskegon River far below the city in a valley, then you ought to come to say you've roomed at a shack. **The Shack,** to be specific. It doesn't have the most inviting name, but this bed-and-breakfast is far from what its moniker and even its weird location—in the heart of downtown "Jugville," as its ads say—connote. Families who stay here for a night or a long weekend are bathed in rustic luxury, from the beautiful log-cabin rooms, nine with hot tubs inside, to the inexpensive rates, which include full breakfast, dinner, and a 9:00 P.M. banana split. Kids like the beach on Robinson Lake, too. The lodge, rebuilt after a fire in 1945 and added to over the years, is one of the north's surprising secrets. Rates start at $90 per room (single or double occupancy). From downtown White Cloud head 5½ miles west on Wilcox, which becomes West Fourteenth Street; the lodge is at 2263 West Fourteenth. Phone (616) 924-6683 for reservations.

BALDWIN

The legacy of Raymond W. Oberholzer, carved over the decades of his life in the woods south of this small community, is demonstrated in the impressive collection at **Shrine of the Pines,** dedicated to the virgin white-pine forest that once blanketed the state. Over thirty years, Oberholzer, a hunting and fishing guide, gathered tree stumps, limbs, roots, and trunks. Then, using such simple tools as broken glass, brushes, and deer hide, he hand-chiseled and rubbed smooth the wood to create natural works of art in the form of beds, chairs, even chandeliers and candlesticks.

The centerpiece of the display here is a huge table carved from a single stump, complete with drawers. Step outside the log cabin and you're along the fabled Pere Marquette River, where in spring the river's gravel becomes a nursery for salmon, steelhead trout, and native brown trout. Part of the river is for fly-fishing only. The shrine is 2 miles south of Baldwin on Michigan 37 and is open daily May 15 through October 15 from 10:00 A.M. to 6:00 P.M. Admission costs $3.50 for adults and teens, $2.75 for seniors, and $1.00 for children ages six to twelve; call (616) 745–7892.

SHELBY

You don't have to spend a lot for a "diamond," a "ruby," or "sapphire," or other gem at **Shelby Man-Made Gemstones,** in this tiny town near the Lake Michigan shoreline. The company is the world's largest maker of synthetic and simulated gems. It got its start producing industrial rubies to make lasers and then branched out to create crystals for science and other uses.

The synthetic rubies and sapphires are identical to the ones dug out of the ground but are produced at a fraction of the cost. In the fifty-seat theater, you'll learn about the manufacturing process. The showroom is open from 9:00 A.M. to 5:30 P.M. Monday through Friday and from noon to 4:00 P.M. on Saturday. Theater admission is free and the room is fully accessible to the physically disabled. The store is located at 1330 Industrial Drive, minutes off U.S. 31 from either the Hart or Shelby exits; just follow the signs east. Call ICT, the parent company, at (616) 861–2165 for information.

Some sixty years ago on the Silver Lake dunes here, Malcom "Mac" Woods invented the sport of dune buggying when he fitted a Model A Ford with oversize tires and a big engine to travel the sands between Silver Lake and Lake Michigan. The craze he originated carries on across the country—and so does his Michigan attraction, **Mac Woods' Dune Rides.**

The forty-minute "dune scooter" rides in modified convertible trucks take visitors on an 8-mile route through one of the Midwest's largest dune complexes. En route, drivers provide a running narrative on history of the dunes, and at one point zip along the hard sand beach to make sure everyone aboard gets "cooled off" by a wave or two. Rides run daily from 9:30 A.M. to dusk between Memorial Day and Labor Day; from mid-May through the day before Memorial Day and for fall tours from Labor Day through early October, the hours are 10:00 A.M. to 5:00 p.m. Cost is $10.00 per person, with a $4.00 discount for children under twelve. Mac Woods' is 9 miles west of U.S. 31 at the Hart or Shelby exits; call (616) 873–2817. Nearby is **Silver Lake State Park,** where, besides camping at one of nearly 225 sites and swimming, you can run your own registered dune buggy within the designated 600-acre off-road-vehicle area. Exit U.S. 31 at Shelby Road and drive west 6 miles, then go north on Scenic Drive. Call (616) 873–3083 for information.

LUDINGTON

If you can't afford that Caribbean cruise for the family, here's a Great Lakes alternative. Climb aboard the **SS _Badger,_** the only cross–Great Lakes car ferry still operating, for a relaxing four-hour cruise between Ludington and Manitowoc, Wisconsin. The 410-foot _Badger,_ which accommodates more than a hundred vehicles and 600 passengers, features onboard cafeteria service and live entertainment. The ferry runs from mid-May through early October; departures vary by date. The round-trip fare is $55 per person and $90 per vehicle; children five through fifteen cost $25 each, and anyone younger is free. Call (800) 841–4243 for schedules. There's even a citywide **Car Ferry Festival** in mid-May.

White Pine Village—3 miles south of Ludington, west of old U.S. 31 (Pere Marquette Highway)—is a reconstructed 1800s town of twenty buildings on a bluff overlooking Lake Michigan. Events centered around the buildings are scheduled throughout the summer. The attraction is open at various hours from early May through mid-October, so it's best to call ahead, at (616) 843–4808. The address is 1687 South Lakeshore Drive. Nearby is the **Pere Marquette Memorial,** a huge white cross where it's believed explorer Jacques Marquette died. A bit more to the south is the huge **Ludington Pumped Storage Plant,** where Lake Michigan water is pumped to a huge retention pond, and sent roaring back down a 170-feet drop to generate electricity. There's a small visitors display, overlooks (open Memorial Day through Labor Day), and a campground.

Renting a lakeside cottage is one of the most inexpensive ways for a family to vacation, and one of the best places in the area to do so is **Twin Points Resort,** owned by Jim and Barb Husted. There are ten log cottages, with one to three bedrooms each, perched atop wooded bluffs above Hamlin Lake, where there's a large beach and plenty of shallows for children. Twin Points is at 2684 Piney Ridge Road. Follow U.S. 10 into town and turn north toward the sand dunes of

BILL'S TOP FAMILY ADVENTURES IN WEST MICHIGAN–NORTH

North American Snowmobile Festival, early February, Cadillac, (800) 22–LAKES

National Morel Mushroom Festival, mid-May, Boyne City, (616) 582–6222

National Cherry Festival, early July, Traverse City, (616) 947–4230

Muskegon Air Fair, mid-July, Muskegon Airport, (800) OK–AIRSHOW

Summer Arts Festival, summer, Interlochen, (616) 276–7141

Mackinac Bridge Walk, Labor Day, Mackinac Bridge, (616) 436–5664

Ludington State Park, onto Michigan 116. Go about 4 miles to Piney Ridge Road, turn east, and watch for the sign. Call (616) 843–9434 to reserve a cottage.

Downtown fun in Ludington includes a beautiful city beach and, along U.S. 10, great made-on-the-premises ice-cream treats at the **House of Flavors** (616–845–5785). Shopping includes browser-friendly stores like **Small World Trading Company,** at 202 South James (616–845–0225), which specializes in unusual imports, and **Fort Daul,** 101 West Ludington Avenue (U.S. 10), the quintessential souvenir shop, where you can check out the latest in cedar boxes (call 616–843–2890). At the harbor you can book a charter for **salmon and steelhead fishing** on the big lake. For information on the area, call the Ludington Convention and Visitors Bureau at (800) 542–4600 or (616) 845–0324.

MANISTEE

A city that prides itself on its beautiful **Victorian-era downtown** (listed on the National Register of Historic Places), Manistee is surely one of the most charming towns in the nation. Blocks of its quaint buildings are lit by antique-style streetlamps, and street fests take place throughout the year, including the **National Forest Festival,** held in late-June through July Fourth, with parades, dances, a midway, and fireworks over Lake Michigan.

In summer seven historic buildings are open for tours, including the **Manistee Fire Hall,** at 281 First Street, an 1888 Romanesque building that's one of the oldest in the state. Later on there's the **Victorian Port City Festival,** the weekend after Labor Day. Among its highlights are an antique- and classic-car show, Native American arts and dance performances, a big fish- ing tournament on Lake Michigan—Manistee is also one of the lake's prime salmon- and trout-fishing charter ports—and an arts-and-crafts fair. Take a stroll on the city's **Riverwalk,** a nearly mile-long path along the lower Manistee River in town, or board one of the **Manistee Trolleys** for a narrated tour. At the historic **Ramsdell Theater,** tour the main house or take in one of the plays performed here April through December.

If you want salmon, Manistee has got 'em. More than a dozen charter boats operate in the area, and at a **fish weir** on the Little Manistee River, you can watch Michigan Department of Natural Resources workers harvest fish eggs from salmon and steelhead for later planting. Nearby sites to explore include **Orchard Beach State Park.**

To reach Manistee just follow U.S. 31 into town. For Ramsdell Theater show and tour schedules, call (616) 723–7188. For trolley information call (616) 723–6525. Orchard Beach State Park is 2 miles north of Manistee on Michigan 110; call (616) 723–7422. Information about fall foliage tours, his- toric-building tours, walking tours, other things to see and do in the area is available through the Manistee Chamber of Commerce; call (616) 723–2575.

CADILLAC

Founded on lumbering, this city along Lakes Mitchell and Cadillac is a year- round resort. In summer, campers fill **Mitchell State Park** on Lake Cadillac nearly every night. It has beaches on both lakes. In the downtown **city park** looking over Lake Cadillac is an antique Shay locomotive used during the lum- ber era. Come winter the annual **snowmobile festival** in early February brings thousands to roam the hundreds of miles of trails nearby. Skiers head for **Caberfae,** 12 miles west along Michigan 55, for downhill action, or to the **Manistee National Forest** for cross-country trails. Call Mitchell State Park— on Michigan 115 at the city's west edge—at (616) 775–7911. For ski condi- tions call Caberfae at (616) 862–3333 or (616) 862–3301. For other visitor information call the Cadillac Chamber of Commerce at (616) 775–9776.

THOMPSONVILLE

It's you against you around each gate, dipping your shoulders and letting your skis run, all in the hopes of a medal at the finish. Sound like the Olympics? It happens every day at **Crystal Mountain Ski Area,** just north of Thompsonville along Michigan 115. Your entire family can taste the thrill of downhill racing at any ski resort participating in NASTAR recreational racing, and Crystal is one of the most popular places in the state to do it. The beauty is, you don't have to be an expert.

Regardless of age or ability, you can compete using a handicap system against others in your age group (there are twelve categories, from four years old to seventy-plus) down a course that won't even give beginners a problem. At season's end two skiers from each area go to the national finals. Besides racing, Crystal prides itself on its family atmosphere, with indoor and outdoor pools, great accommodations, and slope variety. In summer it boasts twenty-seven holes of golf. For conditions call (616) 378–2000.

BENZONIA/FRANKFORT/ ELBERTA/HONOR

A fantastic beach, great accommodations, and super salmon fishing make this cluster of small towns along U.S. 31 a vacation winner. Stop first at **Gwen Frostic Prints** in Benzonia. The famous nature artist creates stationery and other items amidst a 285-acre wildlife sanctuary. A large store sells what the back shop makes. It's 2 miles west of U.S. 31 on River Road and is open daily 9:00 A.M. to 5:30 P.M. from early May through early November, and from 9:00 A.M. to 4:30 P.M. the rest of the year. Call (616) 882–5505 for informationn.

At Elberta, if you know how to fish steelhead, you're a "scum." Floyd Ikens of the **Elberta Sport Shop,** just across the lake from Frankfort, takes anglers into the lake starting in June to search for the lake-run rainbow trout under what anglers have termed the "scum line"—tiny rivers of bugs and other debris that signal different water temperatures where steelhead themselves like to fish. Above the water, from Frankfort Airport, you can take to the skies in a motorless craft from the **Northwest Michigan Soaring Club.** Glider rides over the lake last twenty-five minutes. Cost per person is $35 and $45 for 3,000- and 4,000-foot flights, respectively; call (616) 352–9160. For fishing charter information call Ikens at (616) 352–4434, and for information about where to stay in the area, call the Frankfort Chamber of Commerce at (616) 352–7251.

Honor hosts the annual **National Coho Festival** in late August to celebrate the first release of salmon into the Great Lakes here into the Platte River in the late 1960s. The **Platte River State Fish Hatchery,** east of town along U.S. 31, is open for self-guided tours, and in fall, families can watch as thousands of salmon darken the river bottom at the hatchery; call (616) 325–4611.

INTERLOCHEN

Every summer since 1928, talented young persons from across the nation have converged on this wood-shrouded campus to learn from the best teachers music has to offer. The **National Music Camp** was established by an arts teacher, who also founded a full-time arts academy at Interlochen in 1962. Performers like pianist Van Cliburn, who once studied here, come back to teach students and play. The **Interlochen Summer Arts Festival** features nearly 800 concerts with student performers. There are three concert venues, and visitors can also sit in on classes, rehearsals, and impromptu performances on the grounds of the 1,200-acre campus. Interlochen is on Michigan 137 south of the U.S. 31 intersection. Call (616) 276–7200 for ticket information or (616) 276–7141 for general information.

GLEN ARBOR/EMPIRE/CEDAR

Roll or run down a giant sand dune or trek across it and learn how it got there. It's all waiting at **Sleeping Bear Dunes National Lakeshore.** Named by Native Americans who said one of the hulking formations was actually a slumbering bear, the dunes are among the largest freshwater sand piles in existence, rising to nearly 500 feet. At the visitors center, find out how they were formed; then head for the dune slide, where you can make the climb to the top and have fun coming back down. Before you go, tour the 7-mile **Pierce-Stocking Scenic Drive,** with overlooks on Lake Michigan. For more information call the headquarters in Empire at (616) 326–5134. Some of the dunes are now covered by trees, and you can ski on them at **Sugar Loaf Resort ski area,** just to the east, near Cedar. Call (616) 228–5461 for conditions and lodging.

LELAND

The most remote part of the Sleeping Bear Dunes National Lakeshore, **North and South Manitou Islands** are reached by ferry from Leland, fishing-village-turned-tourist-town. According to a Native American legend, the islands are the cubs of the mother bear that became Sleeping Bear Dune and she eternally waits for them to come ashore. The islands feature primitive hiking and campgrounds, and South Manitou has a restored 1839 U.S. Coast Guard lighthouse, as well as one shipwreck. Don't forget your bug repellent. In Leland, shop for smoked fish at **Carlson's** or book a fishing charter in the restored **Fishtown** area. For island transportation tips and other information, call (616) 256–9061. South of the town along Michigan 22 is the first of the area's vineyards, **Good Harbor.** It has self-guided tours and a tasting and sales room. Call (616) 256–7165 for hours of operation, which vary by season.

The whole family will love climbing the massive dunes at Sleeping Bear Dunes National Lakeshore. (Photo by Robert Brodbeck)

TRAVERSE CITY

This rapidly growing city has become *the* spot to vacation for many Michigan families. With great shopping downtown and plenty of waterfront accommodations on East and West Grand Traverse Bays, it's no wonder.

Despite creeping urban sprawl, the environs are still America's tart-cherry capital. **Amon Orchards** in Williamsburg, just north of the city, offers visits to its tree lots both to handpick the fruit and to see how it's done commercially. There's also a market. It's 2 miles north of Acme on U.S. 31; call (616) 938–9160. The cherry harvest coincides with the **National Cherry Festival,** in early July. For information call (616) 947–4230.

Your kids can stand halfway between the equator and the North Pole at the **Old Mission Peninsula Lighthouse.** It's a highlight of a 37-mile drive on Michigan 37 north. The region also has evolved into a major wine-producing area that boasts several vineyards. The largest is **Leelanau Wine Cellars** (616–386–5201). Others include what might be the smallest **L. Mawby** (616–271–3522), as well as **Château Grand Traverse** (616–223–7355), **Boskydel** (616–256–7272), **Bowers Harbor** (616–223–7615), and **Château Chantal** (616–223–4110), which also features bed-and-breakfast stays. Call each winery for directions and hours.

On Grand Traverse Bay's west arm, try a cruise on the **Tall Ship** *Malabar,* which in summer plies the northern lakes during the day, and makes evening sunset trips, too. The 105-foot ship is one of the Great Lakes' largest sailing crafts. For cruise schedules call (616) 941–2000.

Traverse City is at the intersection of Michigan 72 and U.S. 31. Accommodations include **Grand Traverse Resort,** the north's largest, with swimming, golf, racquet sports, and more. Call (616) 938–2100 for reservation information. For general information call the local convention and visitors bureau at (616) 947–1120 or (800) TRAVERS.

BELLAIRE

Besides being a great area for skiing in winter and golfing in summer, **Shanty Creek Resort,** just outside the town of Bellaire, is fast becoming one of the state's premier spots for mountain biking. Bike rentals are available, and in winter, you can choose skiing at two different ski areas run by Shanty and connected by convenient shuttles. The resort is on Michigan 88, 12 miles west of Mancelona, just south of Bellaire. From Interstate 75, take Michigan 72 west to U.S. 131 north, which leads to M-88 west. Call (800) 678–4111 for information.

BOYNE CITY/BOYNE FALLS/WALLOON LAKE

It happens each spring. Just as the wild white trilliums sprout delicately to cover the forest in greenery once again, morel mania takes over during the **National Morel Mushroom Festival** each May. Pickers from across the country converge here to head for the rolling hardwood hills around Boyne, ideal habitat for morels. It takes a little effort at first, but once you find one their trademark caps with furrows and pockets are easy to spot.

Since there are false morels that some people are allergic to, attend the festival to learn what you're looking for. Guided hunts and contests take place each day. A few miles north on U.S. 131, **Springbrook Hills,** near Walloon Lake, hosts weekend mushroom outings. Springbrook is 4 miles east of U.S. 131 on Springvale Road; call (616) 535–2227. For Boyne-area information call (616) 582–6222.

Boyne Falls is the site of what many regard as the Lower Peninsula's premier ski area, **Boyne Mountain**. In summer Boyne also features championship golf courses. It's just off U.S. 131. Call (616) 549–2441 or (800) GO–BOYNE.

PETOSKEY/HARBOR SPRINGS/CROSS VILLAGE

What more delicious thought can there be to a child than a candy factory tour?

In Petoskey, a great vacation city, they can watch and sniff at **Kilwin's Candy Kitchens.** Tours lasting about twenty minutes are offered from June through August (times vary; call first). Kilwin's is at 355 North Division Road. From Mitchell Street, the main downtown thoroughfare, go east 1½ miles, then north on Division. Call (616) 347–4831 for information.

Shop or browse the stores in Petoskey's historic **Gaslight District.** Then head north on U.S. 31 through the **Bayview** area, past magnificent turn-of-the-century Victorian summer homes and marvelous bed-and-breakfasts and inns. Turn north on **Michigan 119** for a scenic drive you'll never forget. Once out of Harbor Springs, site of more shopping, you'll find **Petoskey State Park,** which has beachside camping, and, a little farther up the road, **Boyne Highlands** and **Nub's Nob,** two downhill ski areas. Then you'll discover why state residents have many times voted Michigan 119 to be Michigan's most scenic highway. With breathtaking overlooks on bluffs high above blue Lake Michigan, the roadway is nicknamed the **"Tunnel of Trees"** because of the thick foliage.

Stop at the **Legs Inn** (616–526–2281) in Cross Village, where from mid-May to mid-October some of the best Polish and other ethnic food is served in a rustic setting. It's open from noon to 9:00 P.M. weekdays, and from noon to 1 A.M. on weekends. Via a different route, Cross Village is 20 miles west of the C-66 exit on Interstate 75. For information on the scenic drive and the surrounding region, call the Petoskey/Harbor Springs/Boyne County Visitors Bureau at (800) 845–2828.

MACKINAW CITY

Ask even a local here why the island is spelled "Mackinac" but the city is "Mackinaw" and he or she probably won't know (they're both "pronounced Mackinaw"). The answer is lost with the 300-odd years since the first European settlers arrived here. Three beautiful state parks and a lot of other fun await in this town that comes alive in summer and nearly closes down in winter.

Under the southern ramp of the Mackinac Bridge is the restored old **Fort Michilimackinac,** used by the French, then the British, until a larger, more defensible fort on Mackinac Island was completed. Interpretive programs in summer tell about life at the fort in the seventeenth century.

Four miles south of the city along U.S. 23 is the 600-acre **Mill Creek State Historic Park,** site of a 200-year-old settlement that was discovered in 1972. Beyond the visitors center is a working replica of an eighteenth-century sawmill. There are also several miles of nature trails.

Stay in the city at one of scores of motels or rent a rustic cabin at **Wilderness State Park,** about 12 miles west of Mackinaw City. Six trailside

Terrific shops and restaurants await in downtown Mackinaw City. (Photo by Robert Brodbeck)

cabins (and three group-style bunkhouses) are reached by short hikes. They don't have electricity and are equipped with a woodstove for cooking and warmth, a hand pump for water, and a pit toilet. Cabins rent for $30.00 per night, plus a $4.00 reservation fee, and reservations are a must; call (616) 436–5381. Seventeen other Michigan state parks rent rustic cabins and more than thirty offer minicabins with water and modern facilities nearby. Fees at other parks vary. Call (517) 373–1270 for information.

A few miles south of Mackinaw City along Interstate 75 is **Seashell City,** where, besides the "Giant Man-Eating Clam," you'll discover thousands of shells from across the world. It's at Interstate 75 exit 326 (Levering Road) and is open May 1 through October 31, from 9:00 A.M. to 6:00 P.M. through Labor Day and from 9:00 A.M. to 5:00 p.m. thereafter. Call (616) 627–2066 for information. Each May, join other TV fans for the **Soap Open Fanfare** and meet your favorite stars.

And, of course, there's that big structure leading north to Michigan's Upper Peninsula, the **Mackinac Bridge.** From cable anchorage to cable anchorage, it's the Western Hemisphere's longest suspension bridge, measuring 5 miles. The only time you can walk it is during the annual **Labor Day Bridge Walk.** More than 80,000 are led across each year by Michigan's governor. The one-way bridge fare for passenger cars is $1.50. For Mackinaw City area information, call its chamber of commerce at (616) 436–5574.

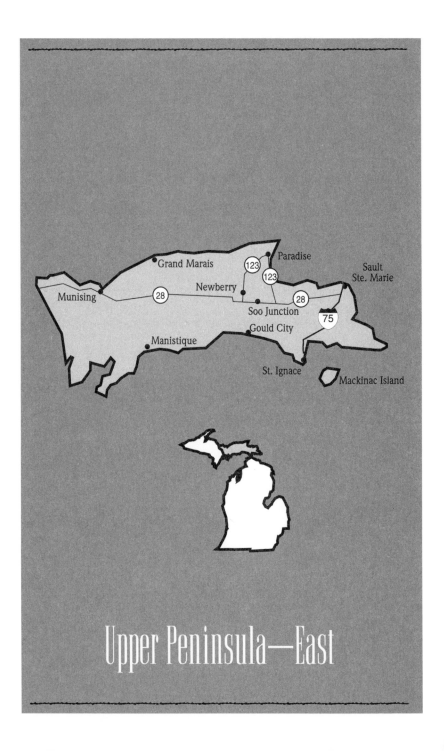

Upper Peninsula—East

Upper Peninsula—East

M ichigan's Upper Peninsula, the UP for short, can be divided into two distinct regions. The eastern part is where farms mix with forest, cities, and other attractions that make this section of the state unique.

MACKINAC ISLAND

Mackinaw City is one of the two spots to catch the high-speed ferry services running to this unique vacation island that formerly was a playground for the rich to escape the heat of summer. Now, the islanders call visitors "fudgies," after its most popular export, fudge.

Tourists in search of cool breezes invade this island (the entire island is a state park—Michigan's first, having celebrated its 100th anniversary as a park in 1995) by the thousands each summer day to walk its streets, ride its bike trails, and enjoy this jewel of a lake.

The pace slows on the island, and except for the clothes, it could be 100 years ago, as the only transportation here are horse-drawn carriages (tours are available), bicycles, or feet. You might want to rent a bike (about $3.50 per hour) and take a 4-mile ride around the island on the only state highway where cars are outlawed. Check out aptly-named **Skull Cave.** Look through **Arch Rock.** Peer inside the quarters at **Fort Mackinac State Park,** dating from 1780.

Other historic spots include War of 1812 battlefield sites, old fur trading posts, and churches. Accommodations range from hotels to cozy bed-and-breakfasts. The gleaming white **Grand Hotel** is the world's largest summer hostelry. And don't forget the fudge, made before your eyes on marble tables.

A ride in a horse drawn-carriage is a great way to see Mackinac Island. (Photo by Robert Brodbeck)

For a unique treat, walk with your family past more than 350 fluttering beauties in seventy species that will land on your family and flit about the **Mackinac Island Butterfly House,** a greenhouse exploding with up to seventy-five types of plants and flowers that keep the exotic butterflies happy. Signs answer most questions. The facility is one of about only 100 worldwide. Admission is $3.00 for adults; $2 for ages three to twelve. It's open Memorial Day to early October. It's at 1308 McGulpin. Phone (906) 847–3972. For island information, call the Mackinac Island chamber of commerce at (906) 847–6418 or 847–3783.

ST. IGNACE

Fr. Jacques Marquette was a busy guy back in the 1600s, exploring the Great Lakes and the Mississippi and founding two Michigan towns, including this one at the north end of the Mackinac Bridge. Since his first visit, it's changed a bit.

Besides being the other town to catch the ferry to Mackinac Island, St. Ignace hosts lots of special events. On the last full weekend of June each year, you can see old-car aficionados caravaning along the highways leading to the town during one of the state's largest street auto shows. **The Straits Area Antique Auto Show** literally takes over the entire town, as more than 2,000 antique and custom Fords, Chevrolets, Studebakers, and the like line up to be ogled. Avoid the hassle of finding a parking spot by heading for the free parking lot and taking a shuttle for $1.00. Another waterfront car show is in mid-September.

To the west along U.S. 2, it wasn't mountain men or other buckskinned explorers but priests who struck out in canoes to explore in the sixteenth and seventeenth centuries, and the **Father Marquette National Memorial** is dedicated to one of the best-known of these missionaries. Artifacts at the site include longhouses and canoes used by the tribes he went among. Video presentations tell the story of Marquette himself. During French Heritage Days, French colonial life is re-enacted. Another site of interest is the waterfront **St. Ignace City Park,** which includes a historical marker on Straits-area shipwrecks. For Marquette Memorial information, call (906) 643–9394.

Downtown, a simple marker is thought to be the grave of Fr. Marquette. Located inside a nineteenth-century church, **Marquette Mission Park and Museum of Ojibwa Culture** tells of the culture of the Ojibwa people Marquette found here when he landed. It's at 500 North State St. and is open 10:00 A.M. to 8:00 P.M. Monday through Saturday from Memorial Day to Labor Day and from 1:00 to 5:00 P.M. until September 30. Admission is $2.00 for adults; $1.00 for ages six through twelve. Call (906) 643–9161.

After the history lesson, head for two tourist attractions that have been here for decades. An ancient lookout used by Native Americans is one of the most inexpensive attractions you'll ever visit. **Castle Rock,** off Interstate 75 at Exit 348 north of downtown, features a nearly 200-foot-tall limestone formation to climb, as well as a souvenir shop. Admission is just 25 cents per person. It's open 9:00 A.M. to 9:00 P.M. May 1 to October 15. Call (906) 643–8268. The other is the **Mystery Spot,** one of the region's first tourist draws that still brings in the curious (some would say gullible). Inside, see where the laws of physics are supposedly turned upside down by clever use of gravity and optical illusions. The kids will get a lesson in science and in the line made famous by P.T. Barnum. It's along U.S. 2, 5 miles west of the bridge, and is open 8:00 A.M. to 9:00 P.M. daily from early May through Labor Day and from 9:00 A.M. to 7:00 P.M. until late October. Admission is $4.00 for adults, $3.50 for ages five through eleven; children under five are free. Call (906) 643–8322. For general information, call the St. Ignace Area chamber of commerce at (906) 643–8717.

SAULT STE. MARIE

Commonly called The Soo, this city was founded by Marquette. Michigan's oldest city, it is now one of the state's most popular destinations for its natural and mammoth man-made attractions.

Here's the first. For a real family treat, see the giant Soo Locks up close and personal aboard the **Soo Locks Boat Tours.** Two-hour trips leave from two locations along the swift St. Marys River and travel up to and through the locks. Captains narrate as you travel, explaining the history of how the raging

St. Marys Rapids, dropping Lake Superior waters 22 feet into Lake Huron, forced ships to portage around the rapids on rails, and how the locks evolved from a wooden structure in 1855 to the longest in the world, handling 1,000-foot-long Great Lakes freighters. You'll drift by giant Canadian steel mills and past the Canadian shoreline before returning. Ships depart mid-May through October starting at 9:00 A.M. Cost is $12.00 for adults; $11.50 for seniors; $8.50 for ages thirteen through eighteen; $5.00 for ages five through twelve. Call ahead for times of the last trip. Locations are 515 and 1157 East Portage Avenue. Call (906) 632–6301, or (800) 432–6301.

Near one of the boat tour docks, step inside the bowels of a real Great Lakes freighter that sailed through seas both calm and fierce for nearly a half-century. Launched in 1917, the 550-foot-long **Valley Camp** is now in permanent dockage on the St. Marys River to teach youngsters what life was like on the decks of one of the great ships that pass through the locks nearby.

Tours take groups from the decks to the iron ore hold and the engine room, where air temperatures routinely ran more than 100 degrees in summer. Exhibits include Great Lakes fish aquariums and two battered lifeboats from the ore freighter *Edmund Fitzgerald,* which sank in November 1975 not too far away, with loss of all hands. The ship is open mid-May to mid-October. Hours vary by month. Admission is $5.59 for adults; $3.50 for ages six through sixteen. Call (906) 632–3658.

For another look at the river, tour the **River of History Museum,** dedicated to the waterway that should have had its own clarion long ago. This attraction will hold the entire family's attention, including antsy kids who think they'd rather go elsewhere. Using state-of-the-art technology, the museum galleries re-create the story of the St. Marys River, used for centuries by Native Americans as a highway and a supermarket. When French voyageurs and Jesuit priests came upon the boiling rapids, they found fishing villages where Native Americans summered, catching their fill of whitefish and trout.

Walk the blue carpet simulating the river and you'll break light beams that turn on exhibits, from a simulated 16-foot-high glacial wall of ice, complete with sounds of crunching ice and rock, to sounds and scenes of later days when crews carved out the giant locks to create the busiest locks system in the world. It's at 209 East Portage in the restored federal courthouse. The museum is open Memorial Day weekend through October 15. Hours are 10:00 A.M. to 5 P.M. Monday through Saturday; noon to 5:00 P.M. on Sunday. Admission is $2.50 for adults; $1.75 for seniors, $1.25 for ages five through sixteen. Family passes are available. Call (906) 632–1999.

See the locks up close from the riverside **Locks Information Center in Locks Park Historic Walkway.** Step up alongside the concrete ditches and

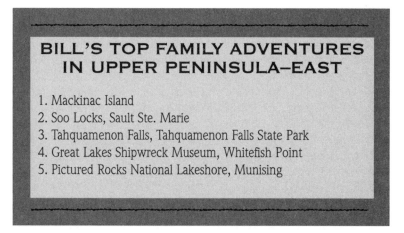

BILL'S TOP FAMILY ADVENTURES IN UPPER PENINSULA—EAST

1. Mackinac Island
2. Soo Locks, Sault Ste. Marie
3. Tahquamenon Falls, Tahquamenon Falls State Park
4. Great Lakes Shipwreck Museum, Whitefish Point
5. Pictured Rocks National Lakeshore, Munising

watch as ships inch their way inside, then are either raised or lowered, without pumps, to the level of Lake Superior or Huron. For more information on the area, call the Sault Ste. Marie chamber of commerce and Convention and Visitors Bureau at (906) 632–3301 or (800) 647–2858.

On the same block, take a tram ride past the city's historical buildings and other sites during a one-hour trip on the **Soo Locks Tour Train.** The trip also will take you across the International Bridge for a short trip into Canada. Tours leave from 315 West Portage Avenue. Memorial Day through early October. Fare is $4.75 for adults; $3 for ages six through sixteen. Call (906) 635–5241 or (800) 387–6200.

SOO JUNCTION/HULBERT

See the falls that inspired Longfellow's epic, "Hiawatha," either by car or all-day adventures that combine trains and riverboat rides. Near this map dot town is an excursion lovingly nicknamed the **Toonerville Trolley and Riverboat Ride.** The 6.5-hour trip combines a 5.5-mile, 35-minute railroad trip aboard the narrow-gauge train hauling up to 250 persons, followed by a 21-mile river cruise accompanied by narration and lots of wildlife from beaver to deer. After the boat docks, it's a short hike to the upper falls, where 50,000 gallons of tea-colored water spews over the lip each second. At 100 feet high, it's Michigan's largest falls and the second largest east of the Mississippi. It's one of nearly 150 waterfalls in the Upper Peninsula. Fare is $15 for adults and $7 for ages six through fifteen, but the rates are subject to change. Cruise times vary, so call (906) 876–2311 for schedules. It's open mid-June through mid-October. Soo Junction is just north of Michigan 28, east of Newberry.

Another water route is aboard the **Tom Sawyer River Boat and Paul Bunyan Timber Train,** which reverses the process. Board from Slater's Landing, 10 miles north of Hulbert for a 4.5-hour river trip and a "train" ride along a path, with the Upper Falls again waiting at the end. The fare is $14 for adults; $7 for ages five through fifteen, and $12 for seniors. Daily schedules also vary by month, but the business operates from Memorial Day to mid-October. Hulbert also is north of Michigan 28, east of Newberry. Call (906) 876–2331 or (800) 732–2331.

You can also just drive to see both the Upper and the cataract-like Lower Falls at **Tahquamenon Falls State Park,** where camping is available at 180 sites near the falls and another 130 sites in its rivermouth unit along Lake Superior. Parking is available a short walk from both falls. The park is on Michigan 123 between Paradise and Newberry. Call (906) 492–3415.

PARADISE/WHITEFISH POINT

A former lighthouse that guided ships past Whitefish Point, 20 miles north of Tahquamenon Falls, is now the **Great Lakes Shipwreck Museum,** a haunting tribute to the more than 5,000 ships that ventured onto what explorers called the Great Northern Seas, never to make port.

To the eerie words of Canadian Gordon Lightfoot's "The Wreck of the *Edmund Fitzgerald,*" you'll see exhibits on many of the ships claimed by the lake's storms. From the wreck of the sailing schooner *Invincible* in 1816, to the loss of the *Fitzgerald* with twenty-nine hands only a few miles west, your family will get a feel of what fury the lakes can hold and how even saltwater sailors fear them in bad weather. The nearby working lighthouse is the oldest on Lake Superior, guiding ships around the point since 1849. The museum is just north of Paradise. It's open 10:00 A.M. to 6:00 P.M. daily, May 15 through October 15. Admission is $5 for adults and $3.50 for ages twelve and under. Family passes are $16. Call (906) 635–1742 for exhibit updates.

GOULD CITY

Want to teach your kids some Michigan history while having fun? It's not that difficult. Head to **Michihistrigan,** a unique miniature golf course 65 miles west of the Mackinac Bridge along U.S. 2.

Owner Fred Burton began building a cartoon-themed mini-golf course, but he changed his theme when he spilled some clay onto some ice in winter and the more he added to it, the more it looked like a part of the Lower Peninsula. The theme stuck, and so did the weird name, coined by Burton and

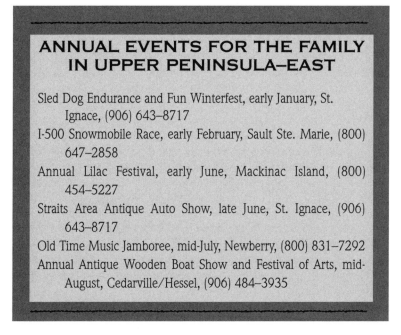

ANNUAL EVENTS FOR THE FAMILY IN UPPER PENINSULA–EAST

Sled Dog Endurance and Fun Winterfest, early January, St. Ignace, (906) 643–8717

I-500 Snowmobile Race, early February, Sault Ste. Marie, (800) 647–2858

Annual Lilac Festival, early June, Mackinac Island, (800) 454–5227

Straits Area Antique Auto Show, late June, St. Ignace, (906) 643–8717

Old Time Music Jamboree, mid-July, Newberry, (800) 831–7292

Annual Antique Wooden Boat Show and Festival of Arts, mid-August, Cedarville/Hessel, (906) 484–3935

his brainstorming wife. Using aerial photos of the state, he built a scale model over thirty acres. While you play, learn the history behind the towns after which each of the eighteen holes are named. At the nineteenth hole, fish for (or feed by hand) the stocked rainbow trout in the "Great Lakes" around the course, then have dinner in the restaurant. There's also a campground, and Burton's latest project is an eighteen-hole, par 72 full-size golf course. The campground, cabins, and restaurant are open year-round (there's also snowmobile trail access); the course is open late May to late September. The cost of a mini-golf round is $4 per person. Call (800) 924–8873.

GRAND MARAIS/MUNISING

Shaped by wind and water over eons, the spectacular **Pictured Rocks National Lake Shore** can be seen on both land and water. Administered by the National Park Service, the lakeshore encompasses 70,000 acres of wilderness along 42 miles of Lake Superior. Glacier-carved rock and waves and wind have created rock formations resembling battleship prows and castles, in multicolored hues from minerals seeping from the soil and rock. County Road 58 through the lakeshore from Grand Marais to Munising is open from May until the first large snowfall. It's about 25 miles paved and 30 miles of gravel. Drivers can stop at platforms at spots like Grand Sable Dunes and the Miners Castle to look down onto the lake 200 feet below. Three rustic campgrounds plus backpack camps for backcountry hikers are available here. A visitor center is in Munising. For information, call (906) 387–3700.

Also in Munising are two waterborne attractions you shouldn't miss. See the lakeshore formations up close aboard the **Pictured Rocks Cruises,** leaving daily from Munising's downtown harbor, weather permitting. The 37-mile trips last nearly three hours and take you almost within touching distance of the rocks. Cruises cost $21 for adults and $7 for ages six through twelve; children five and under are free. Departure times vary by month, so call ahead at (906) 387–2379. Boats run from Memorial Day weekend through October 10. Munising is along Michigan 28.

A few blocks west, step aboard Michigan's only glass-bottomed boat for a view of three of the 5,000 shipwrecks at the bottom of the Great Lakes on **Grand Island Shipwreck Tours.** The 42-foot boat takes up to forty passengers on 2½-hour narrated tours while also sailing past Grand Island National Recreation Area. Wrecks you'll see include an intact 1860-era, 160-foot-long cargo schooner. The cost is $18 for adults, $7.50 for ages six through twelve; children five and under are free. It leaves at 10:00 A.M. and 5:00 P.M. in June and September and at 10:00 A.M., 1:00 and 5:00 P.M. in July and August. Watch for the signs along Michigan 28, west of downtown. Call (906) 387–4477.

MANISTIQUE

Located inside Palms Brook State Park, Big Spring was called *Kitch-iti-kipi,* or "Mirror of Heaven" by Native Americans, and it's easy to see why when you stare into this turquoise pool of crystal clear spring water. Board the roe-tethered raft with a center viewing area and let the kids pull your family across the 200-foot-wide spring. About halfway across, look down. Some 60 feet below you, huge trout are being tickled by the 16,000 gallons of water flowing out of the boiling bottom each minute, into a river that feeds nearby Indian Lake. Sorry, no fishing's allowed, and there's no camping here. Nearby **Indian Lake State Park** has camping. Other activities include hiking trails and a gift shop. Admission is by state vehicle entry permit, which costs $4 daily, $20 annually. Turn north from U.S. 2 onto Michigan 149 and follow it about 10 miles. Call (906) 341–2355.

Upper Peninsula—West

You want wilderness? It's got wilderness. You want big cities? It's got the biggest in the region. The western UP is a mix of the historic and the present-day, from ghost towns where copper and iron ore once ruled, to modern cities where iron ore still plays a big part in the economy and so does tourism in both winter and summer. This region is what many people think of when they talk about the UP.

MARQUETTE

At the north end of the Upper Peninsula's largest city, **Presque Isle Park** is a jewel designed by Frederick Law Olmsted, the same person who created New York's Central Park and Detroit's Belle Isle. A small road leads around the 328-acre facility perched on a rock outcropping jutting into Lake Superior. At the entrance, you might see a Great Lakes ore freighter tied up to Marquette's huge ore dock where high-grade iron ore pellets are dumped into ship holds from bins. Overlooks in the park are countless. Picnic facilities and an outdoor pool are here as well. The park is at the end of Lakeshore Boulevard. It's open daily 7:00 A.M. to 11:00 P.M., and admission is free. Phone (906) 228–0460.

Now if your family's idea of enjoying winter is cuddling under a blanket with the TV clicker or a good book, Bill Thompson wants to show you something different, with a bit of Jack London thrown in. Thompson takes neophytes to experts on what may be one of the most unusual adventure trips you'll ever experience: an overnight journey by dogsled into Michigan's woods. Thompson, who runs **Side Treks Tours,** will teach you how to handle a dog team even on the one-night tour. Like the characters in one of London's novels, you'll mush into the woods, help set up camp, and, with no light other than

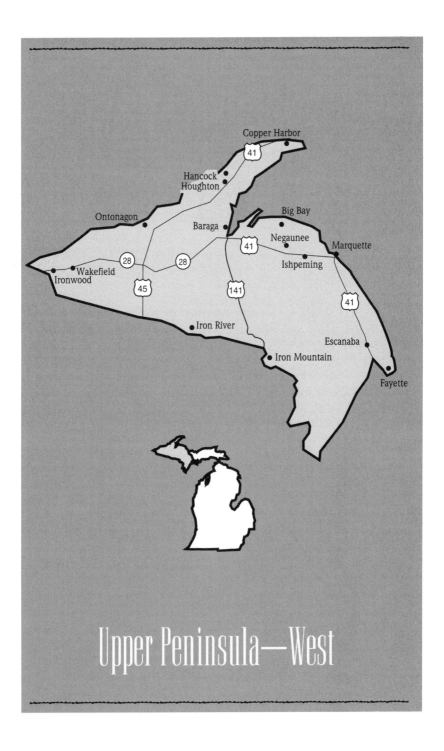

Copper Harbor

41

Hancock
Houghton

Ontonagon

Baraga

Big Bay

Negaunee

41

Marquette

28

28

Ishpeming

Wakefield
Ironwood

45

141

41

Iron River

Escanaba

Iron Mountain

Fayette

Upper Peninsula—West

your headlamp and the fire and despite your probable best efforts to the contrary, you'll learn to enjoy it. In summer, Thompson leads you into the woods on backpack trips or toward the "sea" on kayak trips. Call (906) 288–TREKS (228–8735) for information on the latest trips. Thompson operates out of Down Wind Sports at 514 North Third Street in downtown Marquette. Call him for information on trips and local lodging at (906) 345–9265.

Still other treats in town include a visit to **Thill's Fish House,** where fresh-caught and smoked fish are a specialty. It's behind the landmark **Vierling Restaurant** along U.S. 2/41 downtown. Phone Thill's at (906) 226–9851. Just south of town is **Marquette Mountain ski area;** call (906) 225–1155 for information. For more on the region, call the Marquette County Convention and Visitors Bureau at (800) 544–4321 or (906) 228–7749.

NEGAUNEE

Constructed near the point where iron ore was discovered, the **Michigan Iron Industry Museum** chronicles the life both above and below the earth of the immigrant miners who came to the UP's Marquette Iron Range and two other mining sites. Using a special time-line motif, exhibits tell the range's past from pre-history to the present. Mining cars and other equipment are also on display. Hands-on exhibits for the kids include a model of the Soo Locks and a working model of an ore freighter and loading dock. Hours are 9:30 A.M. to 4:30 P.M. May through October. Admission is free. From U.S. 41, take Michigan 35 south to County Road 492. Go west to Forge Road and turn north to the museum. Call (906) 475–7857.

ISHPEMING

After you've seen the iron museum, you can see where iron ore is still being mined, down and dirty. Ever since surveyor William Burt noticed his compass swinging wildly as he stood atop an outcropping of nearly pure iron ore more than 150 years ago, mining has driven the western UP's economy. Now, families can take daily tours of the giant **Tilden open pit mine.** One of two such operations in the UP, this mine offers two-hour tours that take you from an overlook of the 500-foot-deep pit to the giant refining mill, where ore is crushed and formed in the world's largest kilns into marble-sized taconite pellets ready for rail transport to freighter docks. Tours run from mid-June to mid-August. They leave from the Ishpeming Chamber of Commerce at 12:30 P.M. and from the Marquette Convention & Visitors Bureau at noon. Due to safety concerns, the tour is open only to adults and children age ten and over accompanied by adults.

No open-toed shoes, dresses, or skirts are allowed. Reservations are a must. The cost is $6 per person. Call (906) 486–4841 to reserve.

No visit to the UP is complete without a taste of that peninsular delicacy, the **pasty.** The original UP fast food, pasties are hand-held meat pies filled with meat, rutabaga, carrots, potatoes, onions, and spices. Miners used to take pasties with them into the pits. You'll see pasty signs all over the UP, including the outskirts of Marquette and surrounding cities. Have fun holding your own taste contest to see which purveyor is best.

Now in a dramatic building that's a stylized cross between a ski jump and a Viking hall, the **U.S. National Ski Hall of Fame and Museum** is the nation's monument to its best in skiing. The Hall of Fame honors nearly 300 persons, from skiers to journalists, who've contributed to the sport. Its history section traces the development of skiing, from a pair of skis thousands of years old from Scandinavia through today's high-tech slats. There are video glimpses of early ski races, first chairlifts, and how skis have changed through the years. It's open daily from 10:00 A.M. to 8:00 P.M. from mid-May to early September and from 10:00 A.M. to 5:00 P.M. the remainder of the year. Admission is $3 for adults and $1 for children ages ten through college students; seniors pay $2.50. Call (906) 485–6323.

ESCANABA/FAYETTE

You don't have to travel to the West to see some real ghost towns. About 10 miles from one of the peninsula's largest cities, travel back more than 100 years at **Fayette State Historic Park.** Located along Lake Michigan's Bay De Noc, the former iron smelting town once was home to more than 500 employees of the Jackson Mine Company and their families from 1867 to 1891. Raw ore was brought to the town, where it was refined into blocks of iron called "pigs" in its charcoal-fired furnaces. The pig iron was later shipped down the lake to Chicago, Detroit, and Cleveland for steel-making. Once the trees for charcoal-making disappeared, and larger ships were built to carry raw ore south, the town slowly died out. In the visitor center, a scale model of the city at its heyday will orient you to what's outside. Along with reconstructed kilns and furnaces are twenty restored original buildings. There are eighty campsites as well, plus miles of easy hiking trails at another part of the park. To reach the park, turn south off U.S. 2 onto Michigan 183 and follow the signs about 15 miles. The historic site is open May 15 through October 15. Entry is by state park permit, which costs $4 daily, $20 annually. Call (906) 644–2603.

Michigan is so large we need two state fairs to cover the bounty that the summer brings. The Michigan State Fair, in Detroit, takes place the week before and including Labor Day weekend, while the **Upper Peninsula State Fair** is in

Visit twenty restored buildings at the Fayette State Historic Park and learn how the town boomed from producing pig iron. (Photo by Robert Brodbeck)

mid-August each year at the fairgrounds at the eastern outskirts of Escanaba. Tilt-A-Whirl and tractor-pull fans can get their fill here among the daily entertainment, and plenty of offbeat, family fun attractions make this state fair an exciting event for the entire family, from pig racing to baking and homemaker of the year contests. With respect for the peninsula's heritage, Native American Day is celebrated with traditional tribal dances and other activities. At the grandstand, watch for big-name country and rock stars, as well as motorcycle racing. The fairgrounds are along U.S. 2. Admission is $3 for adults; $1 for ages five through eleven. Grandstand shows are extra. Free parking. Call (906) 786–4011.

BIG BAY

Treat your family to a night like the old lighthouse keepers used to enjoy in the **Big Bay Lighthouse B&B,** unique in the state and perhaps the nation. Surrounded by dense forest and with an unparalleled overlook of Lake Superior, the light, built in 1896, has two suites and five regular rooms. Tell the kids to keep an eye peeled for the "ghost." Don't worry—it's friendly. Then head for town for dinner at the **Thunder Bay Inn,** which was part of the set for the Alfred Hitchcock thriller "Anatomy of A Murder," written by late UP lawyer and former State Supreme Court Justice John Voelker.

You can also treat the family to a four-wheel-drive backwoods tour of the area through Jeff TenEyck's **Huron Mountain Outfitters.** Call the lighthouse at (906) 345–9957, and TenEyck at (906) 345–9265 or 9552.

BARAGA/L'ANSE

Cinnamon buns bigger than your fist await at **The Hilltop,** on U.S. 41, a popular restaurant on the edge of the scenic Keweenaw Bay. Buns are $1.50 each. Call (906) 524–7858. It's 1 mile south of the **Bishop Baraga Shrine,** the monument to the man who worked among the area's Native Americans and was known in the nineteenth century as the Snowshoe Priest. The area's Native Americans celebrate their heritage in mid-July during the **Keweenaw Bay Indian Community Pow-Wow,** with dancing, arts and crafts sales, and more at Baraga's Ojibwa Campground. Call (906) 353–6623.

Just to the north, see the Sturgeon River surge through sheer rock cliffs at the **Sturgeon River Gorge Park** along U.S. 41. The river and falls are a short walk from the parking area.

CALUMET/HOUGHTON/HANCOCK

These twin cities are at the heart of hundreds of years of Upper Peninsula history revolving around the decades when copper was the main export here. When Horace Greeley coined the famous phrase, "Go West, young man," in the mid-1800s, he wasn't talking California. He was referring to the massive copper strikes in the UP. In all, the Keweenaw Peninsula produced more than 8.5 *billion* pounds of copper. The sites here will tell you the story.

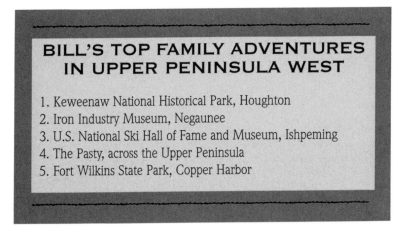

BILL'S TOP FAMILY ADVENTURES IN UPPER PENINSULA WEST

1. Keweenaw National Historical Park, Houghton
2. Iron Industry Museum, Negaunee
3. U.S. National Ski Hall of Fame and Museum, Ishpeming
4. The Pasty, across the Upper Peninsula
5. Fort Wilkins State Park, Copper Harbor

At the core is the new **Keweenaw National Historical Park,** actually a public-private mix of attractions ranging up and down the Keweenaw Peninsula. In Houghton, **Michigan Technological University** is home of the **Seaman Mineral Museum,** on the fifth floor of the Electrical Energy Resources Center. It includes copper and silver extracted from the nearby mines, crystals and even a simulated cave. The museum is open from 9:00 A.M. to 4:30 P.M. Monday through Friday and from noon to 4:00 P.M. on Saturday from July through October. Admission is $4 for adults; $1 ages six through seventeen. Call (906) 487–2572. In Hancock, the **Quincy Mine Hoist** is the world's largest ore hoist, on display at the old Quincy mine. The famed shaft operated from 1848 to the 1960s, producing 300 million pounds of copper. When the last load of ore was hauled up, its shafts had reached nearly 2 miles under the city and Lake Superior. Visit the hoist room, where you'll see the hoist and photos of what it was like working deep in the mine, where temperatures were in the 90s. The shaft house is the area's most recognizable structure, standing 150 feet tall.

You can also step into a portion of the mine worked in the 1960s and then used by Michigan Tech for classes. You'll travel 2,000 feet into the hill to view original workings from the Civil War era, and into the huge stopes, or mined-out underground rooms. A gift shop features historical photos, books, and paintings. The Quincy Mine is atop the hill on the Hancock side of the Keweenaw shipping canal, along U.S. 41. Admission is $3 for adults and children for the surface tours; combined surface and underground tours cost $10 for adults and $6 for children. Call (906) 482–5569, or (906) 482–3101.

For a perfect souvenir, purchase native copper, silver, or Michigan's state gem, the greenstone, at Houghton's **Keweenaw Gem & Gift,** at 1007 West

Memorial Drive (Michigan 26), 2 miles west of downtown. Hours are 10:00 A.M. to 6:00 P.M. Monday through Friday; 10:00 A.M. to 5:00 P.M. on Saturday; 1:00 to 5:00 P.M. on Sunday. Call (906) 482–8447.

Calumet's Coppertown USA Museum is at the core of the new historical park. It acts as a visitor center for the entire Keweenaw Peninsula. Family members can follow the evolution of the mines, beginning when Native Americans extracted pure copper with stone hammers, to the "copper rush" that brought thousands of immigrants to the area.

The Keweenaw gets a lot of winter, sometimes running from November well into May, and Michigan Tech holds one of the oldest celebrations of all that snow, dating from 1922. Its **Winter Carnival** brightens up the campus and is run by students. The four-day event's highlight is the construction of huge snow and ice sculptures to conform with the particular year's chosen theme. The structures extend along U.S. 41 for more than 1½ miles. Be prepared for cold, as temperatures can reach –20°F. Dorms provide convenient warming shelters. The carnival is late January to early February. For more carnival and Keweenaw information, call the Keweenaw Tourism Council at (800) 338–7982 or (906) 482–2388.

COPPER HARBOR/EAGLE HARBOR/EAGLE RIVER

One drive north on U.S. 41 from Houghton, and you'll know why the tip of the Keweenaw Peninsula is, in summer, one of the UP's most popular tourist destinations. Most vacationers save the area for late July and August, since biting black flies and cold weather can be a problem here in early summer. In late summer, you'll find beautiful scenery and lots to do.

For starters, there's **Fort Wilkins State Park.** Built in 1844 to protect rugged copper miners more from themselves than from local tribes, the fort lies along fish-rich Lake Fanny Hooe at the tip of the Keweenaw. It's purported to be the last remaining all-wooden fort east of the Mississippi. Amazingly, it was abandoned two years after it was built, then regarrisoned in 1867 and decommissioned in 1870. Eighteen buildings, twelve of them original, survive.

From mid-May to mid-October, living history workers with help from video presentations and other exhibits portray life in the mid-1800s in this then-remote part of the nation. There's also a modern campground. Admission is by park vehicle permit, which costs $4 daily, $20 annually. It's about a mile east of Copper Harbor on U.S. 41. Call (906) 289–4215.

Attached to the park is the Copper Harbor lighthouse, and the only way to see it is by the **Copper Harbor Lighthouse Boat Tours.** The boat leaves

Attending Michigan Tech's annual Winter Carnival will help keep you warm during sub-zero weather. (Photo by Robert Brodbeck)

the public marina a quarter-mile west of downtown. On seventy-five to ninety-minute narrated tours, you'll learn the history of the town, and visit the light, built in 1866. Take a walk down a short trail to the first copper mine shaft—or at least the first attempt at the mine shaft—in the Keweenaw Peninsula, dating from 1844. Tours run 10:00 A.M. to 5:00 P.M., and the cost is $8.50 for adults and $4.50 for ages twelve and under. Hours vary, and tours are weather-dependent, so call (906) 289–4966. Families can get off the road and step into some of the peninsula's wildest country on daily guided tours and hikes through **Keweenaw Bear Track Tours.** Laurel, Jim, and Hannah Rooks have a variety of trips that'll interest you. Call (906) 289–4813.

Then point your car up. Up **Brockway Mountain Drive,** that is. One visit and your family will know what an eagle must feel like contemplating its domain. Via the winding road with plenty of turn-outs, travel to the top, 700 feet above the town. If you're lucky, watch as passing freighters cruise shimmering Lake Superior. You'll be looking at nearly fifty types of trees and 700 species of wildflowers. The hardwood and conifer mix of trees along the drive makes this a spectacular spot for fall color. On the way down west, you'll pass waterfalls, and roadside parks along the Superior shoreline that are perfect places for picnics or for kids with energy to burn. **The Devil's Washtub** is one of these spots. It's a hollow of rock at the water's edge, which, if the lake's waves are right, becomes a swirling tub of water. Explore for agates at rocky beaches or stop at **The Jam Pot,** run by monks of the Society of St. John, where fresh preserves and baked goods are available from mid-May to mid-October. The Jam Pot is between the picturesque towns of Eagle Harbor and Eagle River on the east side of Michigan 26, next to Jacobs Falls. There is no phone. Accommodations in the area include the Depression-era **Keweenaw Mountain Lodge** on U.S. 41 at the hill above Copper Harbor. It has well-kept log cabins sprinkled around a golf course. Call (906) 289–4403.

Michigan's only national park lies some 50-plus miles off Copper Harbor in Lake Superior. **Isle Royale National Park,** the nation's only island national sanctuary as well, is accessible only by boat or seaplane. But don't think you have to rough it when you visit. True, most come with a pack to explore the island's hundreds of miles of hiking trails and back campgrounds, but **Rock Harbor Lodge** offers excellent accommodations for those without backpacks. Lodge rooms with meals included or modern housekeeping cabins where you cook (bring your groceries with you; the island's store has limited provisions) are perfect for driving travelers. Rent a canoe, charter a lake trout fishing trip, go after panfish and pike on the island's many lakes, or take a sightseeing trip aboard the boat *Sandy,* to see secluded lighthouses and a re-created Great Lakes fishing camp. You can also just take day hikes on the well-marked but secluded trails. Wildlife you might meet includes 1,400 hulking moose (they're more afraid of you than you may think, even if you startle one, but steer clear of cow moose with calves), foxes, eagles, and about fourteen shy wolves. The *Isle Royale Queen* leaves from Copper Harbor from mid-May to September 30 on 4.5-hour trips. The ***Ranger III*** leaves from Houghton on 6.5-hour journeys from early June to mid-September, and a float plane service runs from mid-May to late September. For lodge information, call (906) 337–4993, or, in pre-

ANNUAL EVENTS FOR THE FAMILY IN UPPER PENINSULA–WEST

Michigan Technological University Winter Carnival, early February, Houghton, (800) 338–7982

Pine Mountain ski jumping tournament, mid-February, Iron Mountain, (906) 774–2747

Copper Peak Ski Flying Competition, mid-February, Ironwood, (906) 932–3500

Art on the Rocks, late July, Marquette, Presque Isle City Park, (906) 228–7749

Tilden Mine Tours, mid-June through mid-August, Marquette and Ishpeming, (906) 228–7749

season, (502) 773–2191. For information on the park itself, call (906) 482–0984. For more on Copper Harbor area attractions, call (800) 338–7982.

ONTONAGON

If you're not a Michigander, bet you never thought Michigan had mountains until you read this book. Well, here's another of Michigan's finest peaks. Take a gander off the edge of the rock escarpment at **Porcupine Mountains Wilderness State Park** down at **Lake of the Clouds.** You'll be looking over part of the 58,000-acre park. Located west of Ontonagon at the end of Michigan 107, this beautiful real estate is impressive in any season, but especially in summer when it's cloaked in deep green and in fall when the thousands of hardwood trees mix with pine to speckle the area in red/green splendor. There's hiking, including an easy walk down to the lake shore of Lake of the Clouds or a bit farther to **Mirror Lake** beyond the next ridge. In winter, the park is the only one in the state with **downhill skiing.** Camping is available. Bring plenty of repellent for biting black flies in early summer. Admission is with vehicle permit, which costs $4 daily, $20 annually. Call the park at (906) 885–5278. Call (906) 884–4735 for information on the Ontonagon area.

IRONWOOD/WAKEFIELD/ BESSEMER

The state's westernmost group of cities—farther west, incidentally, than St. Louis, Missouri—only a few miles from one another along Michigan 28 and U.S. 2, claim a particular soft spot among waterfall lovers because of the **Black River National Forest Scenic Byway,** which runs through this area. Of all Michigan's dozen or so Black Rivers, this one is by far the most beautiful. Take County Road 513 from U.S. 2/Michigan 28, and find access, by trails through the woods, to the five waterfalls, up to 40 feet high that this restless river tumbles over in a stretch only 11 miles long. Names like Conglomerate, dropping over a rock ledge, Sandstone, named for the red rock riverbed, and Gorge, which roars into a chasm 22 feet below, are given to the cascades that range from close by the road to a distance along a trail from which you can faintly hear the water. Two of the falls are handicapped accessible, with paved sidewalks. The drive ends at a Lake Superior shoreline park, with a kid-friendly swinging bridge over the now-gentle river. For more information, call (906) 667–0261.

You'll also pass **Copper Peak Ski Flying Hill,** which hosts annual ski jumping events in late January. Several downhill ski resorts are located in this vicinity. For general Ironwood-area information, call (906) 932–1122.

IRON RIVER

This may be one of the most unlikely places for such an event, but professional cowboys from across the country come to this town the third weekend in July for the **Upper Peninsula Rodeo.** It takes place at the Iron County Fairgrounds, off U.S. 2 in Iron River. Call (800) 255–3620 for Iron River information.

IRON MOUNTAIN

Don a raincoat (to protect yourself from the dripping water) and a hard hat to go hundreds of feet below ground through 2,600 feet of tunnels for a glimpse of the **Iron Mountain Iron Mine.** As a guide explains, you'll go by the same train that used to ferry miners into this underground world. The mine is along U.S. 2 about 8 miles east of the city. It is open Memorial Day to mid-October. Hours vary by month, so call (906) 563–8077 to plan your visit.

The city also is home to **Pine Mountain Ski Area** and the **Pine Mountain Ski Jump,** where jumpers from around the world compete in mid-February. Call (906) 774–2747 for information on events and (906) 774–2945 for more on the area. For general UP information, call (800) 562–7134 or (906) 774–5480.

INDEX